The Young Adult's Survival Guide to Living Independently

Life Skills for Getting a Job, Moving Out, Managing Money, Budget Building, Home Making, and just about everything in between

Eli Williams

for all my children...

You've heard me tell you all your life.

"If you think you can, you just might... If you think you can't, you definitely won't." - Dad

https://dadtothebone.com/budgetguide

Contents

Thank You

Dear Reader,

THANK YOU FOR READING!

Thank you for choosing to read my book. If you enjoyed this book and think others will benefit from it. Please consider leaving a review on Amazon. Your feedback helps other readers discover this book. Visit the book's page on Amazon, and click "Write a customer review," and share your thoughts. Your review makes a meaningful impact. Thank you for your time and support!

To leave a review use the QR code or the link below:

https://bit.ly/survivalguidereview

Thank you for your support!

If you're looking for more, you might also like...

https://bit.ly/careerplanningblueprint

Introduction

So, you're ready to move out? You're going to take on the world? You've been under the rule of your parents for so long that you're ready to show the world you don't need to be taken care of any longer. You are the master of your domain. You dream of how you would do things differently or better than your parents. You will do things when you want and how you want, but you're not quite sure how to get started.

That's how I was many, many years ago. I thought I was ready to take on the world. I graduated high school at seventeen and didn't want to be under the rule of my parents any longer, so I moved out of my child-hood home with absolutely nothing but the clothes on my back and an old hand-me-down beat-up 1985 Plymouth horizon. Looking back, I would have done so many things differently. I wish I had started my life more prepared and more knowledgeable about the world. But I was too headstrong to listen to good advice. I've made a lot of needless mistakes along the way, but with every mistake and failure came growth and knowl-edge. Now, I'm a father of three boys and one girl. With the help of my wife of twenty-plus years, we've raised these young adults the best we could to prepare them for life on their own. At the time I'm writing this book, my oldest boy has just finished college, my daughter is just starting college, the third boy in line is finishing high school, and my last runner-up always watches what his older siblings do to make sure he makes better decisions for himself. They are all starting to take their own paths in life, and in doing so, we're here to help prepare them for what this crazy world has in store to challenge them.

Maybe you're not sure what you'll need, what next steps you should take, or what you will have to plan for yourself. There are so many steps to moving out and becoming independent and so many different life skills you might not have had to consider or deal with because you've had someone watching out and doing much of life's challenges for you. This young adult survival guide will show you how to make the most out of what little wealth you might have and teach you how to live with more dignity than ever before. It provides valuable insight into how everything from budgets to relationships changes when living independently.

Life's uncertainties and fears plague us all, and it's normal for you to worry about what the future holds. But don't worry; I'm here to guide you through the fog and lead you toward the light. I will show you how to stay out of debt, control debt, manage your money, and live a healthier lifestyle. A healthier lifestyle will improve your attitude, make you feel better about yourself, and lower your health risks in the long run!

This book will give you the perfect tools to help you along the way, whether you're an adult looking for a second chance at life or just a teenager trying to find somewhere to live on your own without dealing with an overbearing parent or guardian.

Financially, it can be overwhelming to live on your own. You might have student loans, car loans, or credit card debt piling up. You might even be underwater in your car or living in an apartment complex that you can't afford, or just starting out and having nothing to work from. This book will provide you with all the information you need to tackle these financial problems and get out of debt for good.

Believe me, I know, I've been there. Having little or no money is not the end of the world, although it does have a massive impact on your life. A lot of times, people think that just because they have too little money, they have to live a terrible lifestyle. Having little to no money can become your worst enemy, but with the knowledge provided here, you'll be able to manage your finances much more efficiently and effortlessly as well as gain some other life skills you can put to good use.

This book will contain many easy-to-follow tips and action steps that anyone can use to become more independent in their lives. It is an essential resource if you are looking for the motivation or inspiration needed to change your life for the better.

This guide will take you through specific methods you can use to handle money when living on your own. First, I have to show you why this is important and how it can improve your life. This is not just a book about how to make money and spend it; it's about improving your life in every way possible.

Since independence is such an important topic in everyone's life, I've designed this book to be a comprehensive guide that helps show you how to achieve self-reliance. It contains many tips and tricks on living the best possible lifestyle for yourself using the information provided. The advice given here will give people of all ages the confidence they need when starting down their future path. Being able to prepare for your future is very important. I cannot stress enough what it feels like when you are not ready for the future and do not have a backup plan when things go wrong.

I have often been asked, "What advice would you give someone who wants to move out of their parent's house?" This book is my answer to that question. It will show you how many aspects of your life change when you go off on your own and how every mistake made can lead you down a terrible path.

Knowing ways to handle financial problems as they arise is essential for your economic well-being. You can gain this knowledge in many ways, and I'm here to show them to you! Whether it be about budgeting, saving, investing, or even buying a car or a house. I'll give you all the know-how needed so you can be successful when dealing with money.

This book will teach you how to make the most of your resources and skills in any field. Whether teaching yourself a new skill or just getting a second job on the side, this book will show you how to maximize your potential and live comfortably.

There is no need to rush through the book trying to get from points A-Z in a few weeks. It is more important that you take the time to read and comprehend each chapter thoroughly and understand it, then take action on your knowledge. The first few steps are always hard, but over time as we get more experience and practice working on them, we will make fewer mistakes and become better people in our own right.

You will learn a lot in this book, and it will only benefit you if you put into practice what you'll learn. You can trust this guide because it offers practical information and expert advice drawn from years of experience with many younger people. I have written it myself after working with many clients in my private practice, help-

ing them transition into independent adulthood successfully.

Chapter One

Kickstarting Your Career

E verything starts when you have a steady income. Finding ways to bring in an income is the first and foremost important thing you'll need to build a foundation for being independent and living on your own. Whether you create your own business, apply for a job, or work on building a career, you'll need to know what expenses you're going to have and create an income that can support you.

If you're just starting out, you probably do not have a work history to be able to create an impressive resume or make 100K a year. You might have a dream of the perfect job for you, and you may want to hold out until you get into the line of work you're interested in; however, there is a chance you won't find the perfect scenario for which you're dreaming. Don't let your ego get in the way of your goal to make money, move out, be independent, and live on your own. Whether you have a college degree, high school degree, or none of these you can still get a good job to make ends meet. You might even need to work more than one job as you're starting out, even if you have a college degree. It's even possible to grow a job into a career you want just by having the right attitude and drive to make it happen for yourself.

When I was seventeen years old and just finishing high school, I didn't have any college education, but I needed to move out of my parent's home. So, I got out there and got a job. Was it my dream job? Was it anything close to what I do today? No. My goal at the time was to move out of my parent's home and start becoming independent. Even today, I've never had a college degree, but I did grow myself into a Vice President of a major software company. I have a wonderful home, a fantastic wife, and four great children. I worked hard at my goals so I could live without the stresses of financial failure and ruin. I did this all from starting in a mailroom of a large company many, many years ago. Sure, I made a lot of mistakes and had many failures and setbacks along the way, but perseverance and the will to not give up helped me forge through tough times to achieve my goals. I'm positive you can accomplish the goals you set out for yourself for the life you desire to have.

I'm here to help you avoid many of the pitfalls that are common for many of us, and I've stumbled into A LOT of them. I'm here to let you know you're not alone and with a little guidance, I will help you avoid many of the challenges in life that you'll come across along the way.

When you're starting out in your job or career, you have to be prepared for having to take what you can get until you can find what you're looking for. What you need to remember about every job you work is a resume builder. It's a way you can show your next employer your work abilities, work ethic, loyalty, initiative, and level of experience to sell them on why you are the best candidate for the job you're trying to get.

While you're working on getting your perfect job that you can hopefully turn into your career, you have to be realistic in your expectations when starting out so you don't get frustrated in three to six months. You need to have a plan and make goals for yourself. You have to accept that you need to start somewhere, and you might have to take what you can get until you find a job that you truly enjoy. Beginners start at the beginning.

Getting started can be difficult when you don't know where to start. Therefore, this book was created to show you all the things that will be helpful when starting out to help you get on the right foot.

Getting started with or without a high school or college degree.

Before you can start creating wealth, you must create a knowledge foundation. The problem is that many people are unaware of the importance of investing in themselves and their education. I'm here to help!

The reality is that having a college degree doesn't guarantee anyone success. It is just a starting point, and it doesn't mean you're going to make loads of money or be able to get the job you want. To build a career, you need to build a strong foundational work ethic and be prepared to outperform your peers. Finding employment can be difficult because employers want someone they can trust and who is loyal to the company for which they work, someone who works hard and won't quit when the job gets tough. You might not yet have a proven track record showing you're not a person who jumps from job to job every few months. You might have to accept an entry-level position with your small amount of experience and limited performance history of how you behave on the job. A person who knows what they're doing is what a company really wants, and most companies are willing to pay for that type of experience.

One thing you must keep in mind is that even if you might not have any experience or the skills required for a certain job, you can still get hired if you focus on your strengths of being dedicated, willing to learn, and to prove yourself if they invest in you. You will need to convince them they will be happy with their decision to hire you. Show them you're willing to start at an entry-level position so you can prove your dedication and ability to grow into the person they need to improve their business. You might not be able to perform every task in the job description, but you can still be efficient enough to do just as much as someone with a higher level of experience. Employers are looking for someone who can handle responsibilities, take the initiative to handle more than just their assigned tasks, and do it with little supervision.

Possibly you've graduated college or high school, maybe you have just a G.E.D, or you didn't finish high school at all. No matter what you have or have not accomplished in your school career, you can still find ways to make an income and be a productive member of society. It's crucial to have the proper mindset when you start finding ways to make income and become independent. Everyone wants to make a lot of money. Many people don't have the patience or the drive to work to make the money they desire.

Many people jump from job to job, chasing a larger paycheck rather than growing within a company to accomplish the same goal. Be careful if you're chasing money like this because what this does is show on your resume that you are not reliable for a long-term job. You could get passed over for the higher-paying jobs you really want because of job hopping.

Job hunting can be a strenuous and long, ongoing process. It can be discouraging when you get passed over time and time again. Don't give up. It's natural not to get offered a job every time you go to an interview. This chapter will cover the various methods and prerequisites that guarantee success in your journey to independence and career. These tools and tactics worked for me and others who were in the position you're currently in, and guess what? We made it! Now it's your turn!

Career-building tips to help you kickstart your career:

1. Internships

Research by The Bureau of Labor Statistics in 2011 shows that an internship is one of the best things you can do to increase your chances of getting a job. The BLS found that those who completed a training program had a 40 percent higher chance of getting hired compared to those who didn't have any internship experience.

An internship is beneficial for many reasons, but the most important is that it will give you experience working in your chosen field. This will allow you to determine if this type of work is what you specifically want and if it's worth pursuing a career in this field. Even if it's not an internship for your dream career, having this work experience on your resume will be a big plus for future job applications and interviews.

Here are some ways that internships will help you in your journey as an employee:

- It provides a relevant experience that can be evaluated when considering hiring permanent employees.

- It provides a hands-on experience that can speed up the learning curve of new employees.

- It provides a platform for all parties in question to evaluate you and see if you would be a good fit for future employment opportunities.

When you get an internship, you'll get hired and be expected to perform as any other employee. Your goal is to impress your employer during your internship so much that they want you to work there full time. You can only achieve this by being reliable, trustworthy, and helpful in all situations. You want your boss to see you as someone they'd love to have working with them permanently. You want to make yourself stand out from other candidates by having a "Can Do" attitude and having the initiative to see things that need to be done and get involved in accomplishing those tasks. Even if they don't happen to hire you full time, this is a great way to build on your resume to show experience and work ethic as well as get a recommendation or positive reference for when you apply for your next job.

2. Volunteering placement

Signing up for an internship is great, but volunteering may also be beneficial if you're looking for a longer-term job. This is especially true if you find a way to volunteer that's related to your field of interest. Chances are that when employers go for help from the community, they want people who are qualified in their field and have a solid commitment to accomplishing the job. Volunteering matches these criteria and will likely be beneficial when applying for jobs that require these skills.

A simple Google search can lead you to many different websites where you can volunteer your time for various interests, such as charities and advocacy groups. Keep in mind that in most cases, these groups are looking for dedicated volunteers who can show up on time and have a strong interest in their mission. This is one way to show your future employer that you have the necessary dedication to start off a career and build it up over time. Once again, this is a great way to add experience to your resume as well as find positive personal references you can use when applying for your next job.

3. Build your network

The more people you know, the better the chances that you'll find employment. This is why it's important to make as many contacts as possible when job hunting. Having a good relationship with your family and friends can help you initially, but eventually you're going to want to branch out and get to know other people who might be able to help further your career.

Many job opportunities are based on recommendations. When you start job hunting, reach out to people in your network to give them the chance to help you. If someone knows about your skills and experience, they might recommend you. You want to establish yourself as someone who is always willing to help when possible and will go above and beyond to provide some service. Asking them if they know anyone who needs your services will more than likely lead to them being willing to help.

Networking used to be much more complicated and less effective than it is now. Thanks to the internet and social media, there are plenty of ways to use these platforms to build your network so that you can start making connections that further your career as an adult.

4. Creating exciting online portfolios
Creating an online portfolio is an absolute must if your career of interest is in the creative field. This can be an arduous task to accomplish if you're not very familiar with how websites work. Still, when you have a website or social media page that's as professional as possible,

you'll be granted more opportunities to show your skill set.

There are plenty of places where you can build a portfolio without spending much money. By putting together your portfolio and showing it off online, employers will see you as someone who is serious about themselves and the career they're trying to obtain. Not to mention, it shows off your capability to work with different software, skills, and topics. An exciting and well-done portfolio might catch the attention of the right person in your field when they're looking for new talent.

5. Put yourself out there

There is an old saying in sales I picked up along the way: "If you don't ask, you'll never get. What's the worst that can happen? They say no?" Don't be scared of rejection. We all get rejected more times than we even realize. Networking is not an easy task and can subject you to some rejection, which is why many people don't do it, which is also why you want to put yourself out. If you don't, someone else will. Be out there as much as possible. Not only will you have a lot of people to talk to about your opportunities, but you'll also have the chance to get feedback on your portfolio, resume, and any other job-related material that could be useful for you. If you're willing to go above and beyond when it comes time for doing work or providing services, then there's a good possibility that you'll find a way to make things work in your favor.

6. Learning new skills: Expand your skills

The ability to learn and grow is something that every employer wants to see in their employees. Showing off this ability will make it easier for employers to see you as someone capable of doing more than what is typically asked for in the position being applied. If you're an individual hungry for knowledge, I assure you it's possible to grow your knowledge and value using the internet as a learning platform. Most all the skills I've acquired over the years were from self-taught internet research, books, and tutorials. There are so many courses out there that will give you the chance to improve your skills, knowledge, and experience.

Just about everything can be learned nowadays. Halfway through my career, I was a sales manager. I started craving a change. I really wanted to get into marketing and web design. I knew that marketing is a different type of sales and I would enjoy a new challenge. I was already a hobbyist artist and computer nerd. I wanted to do something more in line with what I enjoy doing on my personal time. I didn't have extra money to take expensive classes or any college courses, so I bought some books on programming, watched YouTube instructional videos, and found online certifications. It took a lot of my own personal time to teach myself these skills, but once I felt I had a good skill set, I started talking to my employer about my interests and asked to be given a trial shot at some of the marketing efforts that were ongoing. It didn't take long to prove myself, and they saw enough of the skills I had obtained to want to move me into a marketing position. A year later, I was developing and managing the company's websites and tradeshows. One of the things I learned early on is to work for the job you want, not the job you have if you want to keep growing and climbing the ladder for higher income. The more skills you have, the more valuable you are to the company and the more income you can earn.

7. Find a mentor

In every field of expertise, you're going to want to find someone with the knowledge and experience to help you get started in the right direction. This person can be anyone in your personal network who is willing to give you advice or help you out with situations that may come up while working towards your goals. You'll want to find a mentor who can help motivate and drive you toward your eventual long-term career. This will also help build up working relationships over time before landing the first job of your dreams.

Starting somewhere is better than not starting at all.

Don't be afraid to risk trying anything that may help you in your job search and career. You can always start a business, get involved with community groups you're passionate about, or join a local college club to meet people who share your interests. The choice is yours, but the important thing is that you follow through with your plans for the future. You can't just sit back and hope for things to come together on their own. You need to put yourself out there and do the work so you can to make things happen for yourself.

If starting at zero scares you, just don't be afraid to think outside of the box. It's all about making the best out of what you have and starting from a place of confidence and motivation. The most important thing to remember is that it's never too late to begin something new. You can always begin today and make the most of your life if you can visualize your dream. I've changed my career directions and goals more than ten times, and I'll probably change them again because once I've achieved my goal, I make a new goal higher up the ladder and work to achieve it. The only limitation to anything is the limitation you put on yourself.

Resume Creation what makes a good resume – resume tips

While resumes are generally a necessary part of applying for job applications, there is no magic formula that guarantees an interview or job offer. As such, every resume will vary in format and content.

Generally, a resume's purpose should be to ensure that the person with the skills and experience is presenting the right image to employers. It must also be tailored to the employer or position applied – whether it be jobs at retail stores, military careers, or professional offices. Regardless of the job, resumes generally fall under four types: Chronological, Functional, Combination, and Targeted resumes.

Chronological resumes are primarily used to show your work history or professional experience in chronological order and can span for eight to ten years. It starts from the most recent job and position to the furthest position listing dates and responsibilities. Usually, there isn't a need to go back more than ten years.

Functional resumes are mostly used when you're changing careers or graduating college. You want your history to relate to the job for which you're applying. This type of resume highlights your previous work history, skills, and accomplishments relating to the job position.

A combination resume is, like it sounds, a combination of the Chronological resume and the Functional resume. This is the most common resume to build, especially if you don't have years of work history to show.

Targeted resumes are for "targeting" a specific job or position you're trying to obtain. You can create it using the format of Chronological, Functional, or Combination but the one difference is you are listing your skills and accomplishments that prove you are the right fit for the specific position. It also helps when your resume is online, and the search algorithms can pick up on these specific skills to recommend your resume to searching employers.

Job hunting can be difficult, especially when you're a teenager fresh out of high school. It's a solid concept to be prepared with a resume, but what makes employers notice your skills? Having an outstanding resume is only half of the battle. You still have to get the employer's attention to land that first gig.

You want to make sure you stand out from the crowd when applying for jobs. Use these tips and tricks to get noticed:

Have a clean, organized resume - A messy resume is a big turn-off for any hiring manager. Make it easy for them to read and find the information they are looking for at one glance by keeping everything neat and systematic on your resume.

- **Tailor your resume to the job for which you are applying** - Remember, you want to ensure that the human resource manager likes your resume. You want to show them why they should consider hiring you. Don't send out a generic cover letter and resume that could apply to any position. Tailor the cover letter to the specific job you're applying for and if you know who to address, speak to that person.

- **Keep your resume brief** - The longer your resume is, the less likely an employer will take a look at it. They don't have time to read a novel, so keep it concise and easy to read. If you feel like there is something they may be interested in seeing, add it as an attachment.

- **Show off your skills** - Don't be shy to show off your best assets. Make sure the things you put on your resume show that you're qualified for the job and that you really want it. Employers are looking for a reason to hire you, so finding ways to get their attention is crucial.

- **Know your objective** - It is great to have a resume targeted to the job you are applying for, but it is also essential to show them why you want the position. Be specific with each job you apply for and how those skills benefit them.

- **Call attention to the sections** - If there are sections that employers may be interested in, make sure they stand out and grab their attention. This can include making changes in font and overall layout, so it's easier for them to find what they need quickly.

- **Show off your accomplishments** - This goes along with point 5, but if there are things on your resume that you feel may help an employer, make sure they know about those as well. If something you did or accomplished is team or group-focused, then make sure to include that in the job description.

- **Keep it fresh** - Don't send out old resumes for every job for which you apply. Many people keep sending out the same thing repeatedly, but it's not going to help you in any way. Change your resume and cover letter so that you can keep the attention of employers. It's essential to stand out from the crowd in a positive way. If you want them to notice your resume, then make sure it is well written. Don't send out resumes just to get a job - that is not at all what you're trying to accomplish.

- **Follow up effectively** - If there is a job opening and an employer has not responded, follow up with them after 48 hours, thank them for their time, and let them know when next you would be able to come in for an interview or meeting.

Interviewing

A study in 2015 published by the Office of Personnel Management found that only 27% of applicants showed up for their first scheduled interview. Of those who did come in, 24% provided inappropriate attire at some point during the interview, and 21% had a bad attitude and were challenging. It is no question that being well-prepared for an interview is important. However, getting a job can be difficult if you aren't prepared.

The truth is, most employers want to see that you did your homework and that they're not wasting any time with you. The science behind a successful interview lies in preparation and response strategies that give off a positive image of yourself. In an interview, your goal should be to provide employers with information about yourself that makes you stand out as the ideal candidate for their job position.

While it may be hard just to get a job interview, it is extremely important and vital to your success in a job hunt. If you are not prepared to speak intelligently about yourself during the interview, employers can take advantage of this fact and use it against you during your interview.

Even if employers like you and think that you would be an excellent employee or even if they believe that your skills meet their needs very well and thus they would hire you, they will probably go with the candidate that is more interested in what is being discussed at the moment. In fact, studies have found that employers will be much less likely to hire if you are not passionate about what you're discussing during an interview.

Be memorable. You want to be remembered and stand out from the crowd, so make sure to leave a lasting impression on the employer. This can happen through actions like being punctual and on time for an interview or meeting, as well as taking the initiative and asking questions about what they do.

Let's go over some key points to remember during an interview.

1. Do your homework - You should research the employer, the position, and even their culture, so you can impress any prospective employer with these concepts you know about. Do a little cyberstalking, and go to the company's website to learn what they do and the culture of the business so you can ask and answer intelligent questions and sound like you know what they're needing in an employee. Some websites have a list of top management. You can then look up those people on social media sites to learn a little about who you might be dealing with and find common interests or things to talk about. Remember, you are showing off your skills and talents that you will need to form relationships with the people you'll be working with for a long time

2. Be on time - Employers have stated that they are much more likely to hire someone that shows up on time for an interview. How you present yourself in your interview is how employers will view how you'll be if you were an employee. If you waste the interviewer's time and are not punctual, this could indicate to the interviewer you don't care or you'll be unreliable in the long term.

3. Arrive prepared - Make sure you bring in all the necessary documents, like an extra copy of your resume and references. Bring any information or documentation that will benefit you in your interview. It is also important to arrive prepared with questions that you would like to ask the employer about their company and your potential job position and how you can best help them in their business.

Examples of interview questions:

"How would you describe the work environment at this job?"

"What is the company culture like?"

"What are some of your long-term goals for this position? For the company?"

"If I were to accept a position, what is my typical daily schedule likely to be?"

"What are your management goals for this department over the next months/year(s)?"

"What does the perfect employee for this position look like in your mind?"

"What are the growth opportunities and advancement goals I can make for myself?"

4. Be positive - Employers have stated that they are much more likely to hire someone upbeat because they feel like the person is eager to be there. In addition, employers stated that they want candidates who can focus on them during an interview or work shift, not themselves. When being interviewed by an employer, it is important not just to answer questions asked, but also to remember the points and information you have learned so that you can use this new information in your next interview. It's okay to bring a notepad to take notes. Interviewing can be stressful and a tad intimidating. It's easy to lose your train of thought and forget to ask questions that are important to you. Have them written down and add to them so you won't lose or forget important information later.

6. Be professional - Employers want to see that you are familiar with basic conventions of etiquette and manners such as not interrupting someone or making rude comments. If this is the first time you have been in the employer's office, it is important to be respectful and not just jump into the conversation with dozens of questions or information.

7. Be confident - Employers want to hire candidates that can speak clearly with confidence, even if they are nervous. As a result of knowing what employers are looking for in a job candidate, you need to be confident about your abilities, your skills in this position, and the benefits you will bring to the employer.

8. Be honest - Telling prospective employers about your weaknesses and not making any effort to improve them or work on them is not an excellent way to get a job. Employers know not everyone is perfect and not everyone will have every skill they desire. Your attitude, drive, and motivation to learn could outweigh not having the exact skill they're looking for, and you could still land you the job. It will be your responsibility to accomplish what you promise to do if they hire you. Employers have seen many situations where candidates have told them they are interested in a specific position, then when they are hired, they cannot perform their duties and responsibilities.

9. Be respectful - As stated before, you never know who you will meet when seeking employment. You should always be willing to listen to what the employer has to say and make sure you can act accordingly. If the employer is not giving you any hints about your interview, you need to respond in a way that keeps the interview going smoothly, without pushing them too far.

10. Show enthusiasm - As stated before, show that you are enthusiastic about this position and would like to help the company in any way possible. Suppose an employer is interviewing multiple candidates with similar skill level or personality traits. In that case, they will go with a candidate who seems more interested in being there.

These are some points that you should follow when it comes to an interview if you are going to be successful in obtaining a satisfactory job. By following these tips and preparing yourself as well as possible in advance of the interview, you can maximize your chances of getting the job.

The week or so leading up to an interview is a perfect time for you to prepare yourself by studying, practicing your answers, and researching exactly what the employer wants. As you prepare for an interview, there are a few things you should ask yourself. What qualities or traits would make you a good candidate for this position? What ideas would impress an employer? You should also keep any notes about points that the employer has asked for in previous interviews and do your best to address these topics during the interview.

Finally, it is important to have a clear idea of what your strengths and weaknesses are. When seeking employment, it is common for employers to ask candidates about their strengths and weaknesses, so be sure you

have considered this topic before entering any interview.

Chapter Two

Choose a Bank / When and How to Open a Bank Account

With independence comes great responsibility! It is crucial for you to open a bank account and get into the habit of saving money. You should also make sure that you are knowledgeable about finances and banking before making any crucial decisions regarding your money.

Federal law requires financial institutions to provide free information on selecting accounts and understanding bank statements. With this chapter, you will gain some information about financial terms, the various features of a bank account, and choosing the right bank for you.

Financial Terms:

When it comes to understanding banking, it is essential for you to understand some basic financial terms. The following are some of the most commonly used terms:

- **Banking** - The process of storing your money in a physical location that can be accessed through checks or an ATM card by those with permission.

- **Cash:** Can be made out of paper or electronic. It can be in the form of checks, money orders, and coins.

- **Checking Account:** Usually limited to those with a good credit standing. It is similar to a savings account but allows you to write checks. The interest earned varies by bank.

- **Savings Account:** A deposit account in which money is invested and earns interest, often at a fixed interest rate per year. It is similar to a checking account but with no check-writing privileges.

- **Checks:** Negotiable instrument that allows a bank customer to write or draw against their deposit in order to pay debts or obligations arising from past transactions or current events. A check is generally accepted as payment for goods and services.

- **Debit Card:** Electronic card that authorizes a customer's bank account to provide automatic receipt of funds for purchases and cash withdrawals from ATMs. The amount is immediately deducted from the customer's account each time it is used.

- **Overdraft and Overdraft Protection:** An overdraft is a type of transaction that occurs when the account holder's balance falls below zero. That means the account cannot cover regular transactions, such as checks, debit card transactions, and ATM withdrawals. When you sign up for Overdraft Protection, your bank will prevent your account from being overdrawn each month by reviewing your transactions and automatically transferring funds for you to avoid the embarrassment, however you will incur fees associated with an overdraft. These transfers can be set up as one-time or recurring automatic payments that transfer money when the balance drops below a certain level.

- **Direct deposit:** Sends a payment electronically from an employer or other authorized third party directly to your bank account. A payroll check, Social Security payments, and government checks are common examples of direct deposit.

- **Electronic Funds Transfer (EFT):** An automated funds transfer between two financial institutions using the Automated Clearing House (ACH) network. EFTs can be initiated by the customer or by a financial institution for certain services such as prepaid debit cards or wire transfers. The two financial institutions usually are different types of banks, such as a credit union and a bank.

- **Electronic Purse:** Also called a smart card. It is a credit card that can hold bank information. It is used in conjunction with an ATM.

- **Federal Deposit Insurance Corporation (FDIC):** A federal corporation that insures deposits at member banks up to $250,000 per depositor per bank. It guarantees your funds will be returned if your bank fails.

- **Financial Institution:** A financial organization that accepts deposits and offers various financial services, such as mortgages and loans or deposit accounts.

Interest: Interest can either earn you money or cost you money. When you have a savings account, a bank might pay you interest on the amount you have saved in the back with them. For example, a bank might pay you one to two percent interest every month on the amount you have in the bank. So if you have $100 in the bank, you would earn $2 from the bank. It's always a good idea when shopping for a bank to learn how they will earn you income by doing business with them. Adversely, credit card companies might charge you 25% interest every month on the balance you owe them. For example, if you borrow $100 from a credit card company, they will charge you $25 at the end of the month for borrowing the $100 from them.

- **Money Market Fund:** A mutual fund that invests in short-term, high-quality government securities.

- **Prepayment Certificate (PPC):** A certificate issued by a financial institution to a consumer to obtain an unsecured loan.

- **Prepaid Debit Card:** A plastic card that can be used to make purchases using funds deposited into the card or preloaded on the card.

- **Stripe:** A strip of paper recording the transaction entered into an ATM machine.

- **Treasury Bill:** A U.S. government security sold to the public at a discount, buying it back at a later date at full price. Interest earned on a treasury bill is taxable on your federal income tax return, but it is NOT taxable under state and local laws.

- **Transaction:** A transaction is any deposit, withdrawal, any type of work with any account.

- **Vault Cash:** Deposits at a bank not invested in securities

- **Checking Account:** Allows you to write checks but is considered an "unsecured loan" because there is no collateral backing the account. The bank can close your account if you write too many bad checks or checks for amounts exceeding the balance in the account. It earns interest but has a finite balance. If you don't have enough money, then you will be charged overdraft fees for bounced checks, ATM transactions, and other charges to the account.

- **Savings Account:** Is an interest-bearing account with no check-writing privileges.

- **CD** (certificate of deposit): An account that pays interest for a specific amount of time. CDs usually have higher interest rates than checking or savings accounts.

- **Overdraft Protection:** A legal agreement between you and your bank that allows you to overdraw your checking account, but charges you an additional amount every time you use it. These fees can be high and vary depending on your bank and how much overdraft protection you have set up on your account.

- **Personal loans:** When you need extra money to make a large purchase because you do not have the funds to pay for it with your savings, such as purchasing a new car or house, remodeling your home, or consolidating some debt, you can talk to your bank and ask to borrow money that you will pay back over an agreed amount of time. Personal loans are charged an amount of interest you will also have to pay back over that period of time.

- **Business loans:** Business loans are typically issued when a company needs to buy new equipment or expand its operations. These loans are often required for growth and expansion purposes. As long as the borrower can show that the enterprise has the ability to repay the loan in full and on time, then business loans will be approved.

Basics of banking

What is banking?

Banking is a valuable service that allows you to store and move your money. Some banks will provide additional services such as checking accounts, savings accounts, loans, and money transfers. There are also multiple types of banking accounts that you can choose from. Many factors go into choosing the best banking for your financial situation, including but not limited to, bank charges and fees, interest rates, and security standards of these accounts. It is important for you to understand the different types of banking you can do and how they operate, so that you can make an informed decision about what type of banking account or accounts fit your financial needs best.

What makes a good bank?
A good bank should be able to offer many beneficial features. In order to do this, it is necessary for banks to provide the best deposit accounts, best checking accounts, and best savings accounts. These types of accounts are considered better than checking and savings because they offer higher interest rates for deposits as well as a more secure structure. It is also important that banks have a variety of banking services available. This will allow you to choose the right type of account that is right for your situation so that you can take advantage of every feature it offers.

It is important to remember that not all banks are created equal as they have different features and standards for what is considered good banking standards. When you shop for a bank, you want to make sure you have a variety of banking services available. This will allow you to choose the right type of account that is right for your situation so that you can take advantage of every feature it offers.

You'll also want to pay attention to the quality of the customer service offered by the bank. Good service should be based on being able to help customers and work to resolve any issues they might have. There are a wide variety of things that can cause issues for customers, and good customer support is what you'll want so they will help you quickly should you have a question or problem with which you need assistance.

What makes a bad bank?
While there are numerous features that make up a good bank, there are also many features that make up a bad bank. With so many different banks to choose from, it can be hard to know which one is the best for your situation. A common problem with banks is that they have very high minimum deposits and withdrawal limits. This means that you might find yourself unable to withdraw any of your money or close out the account without incurring a large amount of fees. Another common problem with banks is maintaining reasonable banking policies and standards. Some banks might have different policies and rates than those in your home town, so it is important to know if you plan to travel with your bank account. And lastly, having a bad bank means it can be hard for you to take out money. In some cases, banks will close accounts if there is not enough money in them. This can be extremely difficult for individuals who don't have savings accounts or checking accounts to back up their banking accounts.

Realistically, there are many good and bad qualities of banks. It is important that you do your own research before deciding which bank is right for you.

How do ATMs work?
Automated Teller Machines (ATMs) have been around for a long time. While not all banks have ATM machines, most are connected to other banks in order to access funds or credit should your own bank's ATM machine not work. Many ATMs also give incentives to customers by providing cash back when the customer withdraws money from an account that is linked to their debit card. The way ATMs work is relatively simple. Once you enter your code, you select how much cash you want, which will automatically begin the process of printing out a receipt for your transaction. Then, from the ATM machine itself, you can either receive cash or transfer it directly into one of your accounts. Be careful; using an ATM used to be free. Nowadays, ATMs charge large fees to pull money out of your account. So, if you decide to use ATMs often, make sure you're budgeting for your ATM usage fees as they can add up very quickly depending on how often you use ATMs.

What are some good strategies for banking?
There are numerous strategies that you can use to ensure that you have the best bank account. Selecting the best bank is important because it allows you to choose the type of account that you need for your situation.

However, there are other factors to consider when selecting a good bank. You should also take into account interest rates, monthly fees, and annual fees in order to determine if you are getting an adequate return on your investment in the first place. Also, find out what other banks offer. Do they offer similar services and comparable rates as other banks? Lastly, ensure that there are branches close by or accessible through ATMs in order to have easy and convenient access when you need it most. It would also be a good idea to investigate how hard or easy it is to access your account if you're ever traveling out of state for vacations or business trips.

What makes a bad internet bank?
The internet has fundamentally changed how we conduct our daily lives. Almost everything we used to do at a physical brick-and-mortar location can now be done online from our computer or mobile device. Banking is no different. In fact, for many people, banking online is much more comfortable and convenient than going to a physical bank. However, banking online does have its drawbacks. This is especially the case when it comes to internet banks.

What makes an internet bank terrible are all of the features that make it inferior to an ordinary bank. This includes higher transaction costs because of transaction fees and being less secure because there are fewer or no physical branches. Some internet banks will also charge you for transactions that you would normally get for free at traditional banks, such as paying bills or transferring money between accounts. Protect yourself and do your research. What seems like a convenience or a necessity at the time can turn out to be a long-term issue and hard to get out from under. Traditional banks, I feel, are still the best way to go because if there is an issue, you can walk into the bank and speak to a real person or a bank manager face-to-face to resolve issues or ask questions to gain knowledge. It's also helpful to have a relationship with your bank when you need to work with them on a personal or business loan. They know you and are more willing to work with you because you are their long-term customer.

What makes a bank secure?

Banks are obviously trusted by many people because they act as financial institutions that hold your money and credit. When you deposit your money into an account at a bank, the bank then has to take the responsibility of keeping that money safe. Generally, banks have several different ways of making sure your money is secure when it is in their possession. Some banks make depositors feel more comfortable by having vault cash or cash on hand. This means that there is actual physical cash in the building somewhere instead of just electronic records. Rest assured that it's not truly your money sitting in the vault; your money is protected digitally and insured in case there is any theft at the bank.

How does online banking work?

First of all, know there is a difference between banking online and having an online bank. If you choose to sign up and do business with an online bank you can do many things a brick-and-mortar bank can do. The major difference is you can't go to the bank and speak with someone in person. You have to use online chat sessions, emails, phone calls, and hope the person on the other end speaks the same language you do. Banking online can be done in different ways, such as phone banking. Phone banking involves calling a particular phone number, which will then transfer your money into your account and allow you to choose how much you would like to transfer. Online or mobile banking allows you to use your computer, tablet, or smartphone and access almost the same features as brick-and-mortar banks.

What are the advantages of online banking?

On online banking websites, you can pay bills and transfer money from one account to another quickly and easily by doing a few keystrokes on your keyboard. Online banking also allows you to check and track the balance of your checking accounts, savings accounts, brokerage accounts, and possibly your credit card accounts in addition to viewing statements from all of them. With all these features, it's hard not to prefer online banking over going to the bank physically and waiting in line. I would recommend in your banking research to learn what kind of online banking services the bank offers, and have them show you their website to make sure it has all the features you need and is easy to use. One time I had a bank that said they had online banking tools; however, the website looked very old, was hard to navigate, and didn't have all the expected features used by bigger more established banks.

What are the disadvantages of online banking?

Online banking has some potential downsides. One of the biggest disadvantages is that your money isn't secured as safely as it would be when you have it at a physical bank. Online banks have fewer protections from theft than physical banks do. Security problems in online banking stem from two basic issues. The first is the potential for criminals to intercept private data being sent across the internet. The second is the susceptibility of web-based banking to software exploits, like worms and viruses that attempt to gain control of connected systems.

The majority of financial institutions require users to install plug-in software on their browsers called an encryption certificate or a digital certificate or a security certificate for protection against this kind of threat. However, the use of these programs may not be enough. Software flaws in the browser may leave users vulnerable to security attacks.

In addition, virtual bank accounts are increasingly in use, which requires customers to have computer skills and the know-how for managing money online. Although these accounts are convenient for those who lack such skills, they also constitute a risk of identity theft. Banks provide customers with login information and password security through digital certificates, but new-age hackers can hack into these programs just as easily.

Another disadvantage is that some people may find it hard to keep up with the fast pace of doing banking transactions online because it takes time to get used to using computers and mobile devices. Online banking has also been criticized for being too expensive for the average consumer. With the credit crisis of 2008, many banks advanced interest rates on their floating-rate loans to customers without asking. This had a negative impact on the amount of money people had in their bank accounts.

Banks have also been criticized for charging monthly maintenance fees on checking accounts. Typically, banks relinquish money from these accounts to pay for the upkeep of their branches, salaries, and other administrative expenses. However, they used to charge lower fees before the credit crisis of 2008.

In addition, banks have also been criticized for their interest rates and hidden charges that are not made clear to customers in their fine-print policies. For instance, a customer who wants to cancel an overdraft fee must pay a considerable amount of money just to be able to do so. Some consumers might prefer the comfort of going into an actual branch and speaking with a human being face-to-face about their finances. However, if you're comfortable managing your money from home, then an online-only banking experience might just be for you! I recommend doing your research; ignorance of things like this is a choice, not an excuse.

What is the difference between credit cards and debit cards?

Individuals use credit cards to make purchases, but the use of credit cards comes with much greater risks and restrictions than debit cards. Credit card companies do not expect you to pay for everything upfront. Instead, they assume that if there is enough equity in your checking or savings account, you will be able to make payments in increments back to them over a period of time. This way, they can charge you high interest on your purchases based on the value of your purchase.

Debit cards work similarly to credit cards in that they allow you to make purchases or withdraw cash from an ATM machine. However, a debit card spends money directly from your savings or checking account imme-diately. So if you don't have money in the account, the debit card won't work. In order for the debit card to function, the debit card requires you to sign up for an account where you will deposit your own money. This is done via a checkbook-style checking account linked with the debit card and allows the ability to withdraw money directly from the bank at any time without paying fees at ATMs or banks.

Different accounts offered in banks

There are a variety of different accounts that banks offer to their customers. These include checking accounts, savings accounts, gas and oil discount cards, credit card accounts, and checking with interest-bearing accounts. There is no one best way for you to effectively choose which type of bank account will help you achieve your financial goals. However, choosing the right kind of bank account can be beneficial to you in the long term if you use these services properly. As an example, if you are trying to keep up with your student loan payments or paying off an extravagant debt, a checking account may be more effective than a student loan or credit card debt management plan. Banks usually have a financial consultant who can work with you and help you understand the different options they have to offer and will help you make the best decision for your situation.

Checking account and savings account

A checking account allows you to access your funds at any time and can be used to pay your bills or buy goods and services. You will receive a checkbook that allows you to pay for something and the money will not be deducted from your account until the other party deposits your check into their bank account. On the other hand, a savings account is meant for saving money on a long-term basis. This type of bank account is available in many different banks, with some offering a wide range of products you can choose from. Both types of accounts come with varying interest rates and/or bank fees, which may be low or high depending on the bank you choose.

Checking accounts for students

These are simple enough to use but are not as beneficial as regular checking accounts in the long run. With a student checking account, you will have fewer products and choices with your bank, and you will likely have to pay fees for using an account. You should also be aware of interest rates and learn how they work so that you can save money in the long run. This way, your money won't just be wasted when you put it in a checking account without knowing how interest works or why it is crucial. Checking accounts generally do not offer many incentives for students to use them; however, some banks offer student accounts as incentives to go with certain banks over others.

Checking account with debit card

A checking account with a debit card is one of the most basic bank accounts you can have. The only difference between it and a regular checkbook is that you will most likely have your own debit card to use whenever you want without paying additional banking fees.

You can make purchases, bill payments and withdrawals wherever and even withdraw cash from ATM machines, making it easier to access your money on the go. Be careful the easier it is to access your money, the easier it is to spend it. You have to keep yourself disciplined to a budget

What is a savings account and how does it work?

A savings account works much like a checking account. You can have your money deducted from the amount you have accumulated in it. The idea of a savings account is to put money into the account and not spend it. You want to keep adding to the balance and save it. Depending on your bank's offerings, the more you put into your savings account, the more you can accrue interest to the balance. The bank helps grow your balance by paying you to keep money in the account. However, unlike a checking account, this money will not be as easily accessible whenever you need it. If you need money but don't want to pay fees at an ATM, you will have to go to a physical bank to make a cash withdrawal. If the bank is closed, you will not have access to your money unless you have a debit card connected to it, and some debit cards have a daily withdrawal limit. If an expensive emergency comes up and you hit your withdrawal limit from the ATM and the banks are closed for a three-day weekend, you're stuck until the bank opens again.

How much should you save

Putting aside money for a long time is not an easy thing to do. In order to save as much as you can, you may want to consider opening a savings account that offers you a high-earning interest rate. This way, the more you have in your savings, the more the bank will pay you to keep a large sum of money in your savings for a long period of time.

TICs, or tiered-interest CDs, offer something called tiered rates of interest: When it comes to things such as bank accounts, CD rates have been on the rise for the past several years. That's because banks and credit unions have realized that people like savings accounts with higher interest rates rather than traditional checking accounts and savings products, which offer lower interest rates.

Tips on saving

Moving out can be challenging for many reasons, but what can be even more challenging is building a nest egg savings. It takes a little financial planning to start a savings plan for yourself and a lot of self-discipline to make it grow. If you are not used to living on your own, you might not have any idea where to begin.

Make a budget
A budget can help you decide how much money you can give yourself each month to spend on food and other goods. Every paycheck, you may want to take a designated amount of money and put some into your savings account. The rest can go to your checking account or any other financial products that you may have. You may find it helpful to also set up a separate "moving out fund" so that you can save up extra money as getting out of the nest becomes more important.

You can use coupons
Coupons will help spend less. Many stores offer deals through coupon codes. If you're struggling to find an extra dollar or two to put into your savings every month, here's a strategy for using coupons to help you. Consider a product you were going to purchase for $3.00. You were planning and budgeting to spend that $3.00 when you made the purchase. However, if you had a coupon for the product that lowered it by 20% from its original price means you'll save $0.60 on the

purchase. Take that $0.60 you had planned to spend and put it in your savings account as if you spent it. You were going to spend that $0.60 anyway, so keep it deducted from your spending account and put it in your savings account. Imagine if you added up all the savings you could get using 20 coupons for your groceries. All that money you were going to spend at full price you can take that portion and put it right into your savings as if you spent it. Now, you don't have to scrounge money from your paychecks to put into savings. You're just put into savings what you were going to give to the store by paying full price.

Keeping track of your expenses

You may not realize it, but tracking your expenses on a regular basis can help you save money. Many people waste money on monthly subscriptions and services that they don't need and don't use. By keeping track of how much you spend on different things (and then canceling or downgrading non-essential subscriptions), you will be surprised at how much extra cash you can have each month. Ask yourself is this product or service something I must have to live or is it something that is nice to have but I can live without for now?

Ask yourself how I can cut on expenses

The most effective way to cut down on your expenses is to be as frugal as possible. Ask yourself if you really need a bigger apartment or a more expensive one. You can also look for cheaper alternatives when it comes to buying furniture or other large items for your home. Many times young adults have grown accustomed to the luxuries of their parent's homes. You might think you need to have all the same luxuries. But in reality, and more than likely, your parents didn't start out in life with all the things they have today. They started out much like you with very little and crappy stuff that was affordable at the time, and they worked their way over years collecting and developing the home they have today. Give yourself realistic expectations on what you need to survive on your own, and over time you'll save and collect the luxuries you want to have.

There are many ways to cut expenses without sacrificing your quality of life. For example, you can cut costs on cable service while increasing your savings by finding a cheap Wi-Fi service and using less expensive or even free internet streaming services.

Discounted shopping
Some retailers offer coupons that can be used in person at their stores or online. Even Amazon offers discounts for Prime customers who want to save some cash on their purchases. As an added bonus, some discounts are only given when you check out using Amazon's mobile app.

Avoid using your card for everything
If you have to use a credit card, then make sure that you pay the bill off before the end of the billing cycle.

Remember, when you are using a credit card you'll be charged over 20% interest on your purchase if you do not pay off the balance during the billing cycle. This means your $150 groceries purchase is really a $180 purchase and if you do not pay it all off, you'll pay even more for those groceries. This is how people dig themselves into a debt hole before they realize it by trying to pay off their interest amounts on small purchases. Could you imagine paying for a carton of eggs for three or more months? The best way to get out of debt is to avoid getting into more debt in the first place.

Determine your financial priorities
Instead of spending money on new clothes or furniture for your new place, you may want to focus on eliminating debt and saving for a rainy day. It is important that you determine what's more important for your finances and then stay committed to those priorities.

Make saving a habit
In order to save more money, you need to make saving a habit. Whether you decide to put away $10 or $100 each month, just make sure that you are setting aside some cash for yourself before spending it.

Overdraft protection

Overdraft protection can be a useful tool when you have made a calculation error and thought you had more in the bank than you did when you made a payment or purchase. If your card is declined or your check tries to clear and there aren't enough funds to cover the amount, then the bank will cover the amount for you instead of your bill getting unpaid and your utilities getting shut off. However, this protection will come with a cost. Banks will charge anywhere from $15 - $35 on each transaction the overdraft covers. This can quickly become expensive and deplete your funds fast, putting you into a financial hole. Overdraft fees are not unusual, and any financial institution can charge them. In fact, overdraft fees are the second most common source of banking income after interest.

When I was starting out, I would accidentally cause overdraft fees at least once or twice a month. What I realized is this protection was like throwing away $35 every time it happened. So, in my trials of making a budget, I built a $100 buffer and kept this amount in my checking account at all times. This way, I would keep the bank from getting my $35 dollars for free. If I had to use some of my $100 buffer, I would replenish this amount from my next paycheck, but I was able to keep my money mine. Over the years, I started increasing my buffer budget, and now I no longer have overdraft fees or the need for overdraft protection at all. Overdraft protection is a service that many financial companies offer, including banks and credit unions, and can be very helpful when you're just starting out and have limited funds. As soon as you can, make yourself a safety buffer to keep yourself from giving your hard-earned money to the bank for free.

Disputing fees

Credit card companies and banks can charge you a variety of fees if you do not make payments on time. The most common fee is the late payment fee – this is something that many people have no idea they have to pay until they receive the bill in the mail. There are also fees for returning items, applying for new cards, or getting hit with overdraft protection.

Most credit card companies will refund any fees you are charged

Credit cards often come with statements that show any fees that were charged to your monthly payment, as well as how much was refunded back to you. It is important that you report any disputed charges with your credit card company as soon as you are billed for them. The earlier you dispute the charge, the better chance you have of getting a full refund from the company. Be professional and friendly. Explain the situation and why you feel the charge should be waived. You will get more help and have a better chance at accomplishing your goal rather than trying to yell and force yourself on the person who answers the phone.

Make sure you document everything: If you want to get these charges removed from your statement, then you need to make sure that your dispute is taken seriously by the company's representative. Many times you can clear things up with a simple phone call and work with the respective company. In rare cases, should it become an issue, you may even need to hire an attorney and make sure that all communication is documented so that there is no confusion about why the fees were removed.

Make frequent payments: The best way to avoid credit card interest and fees is by making consistent payments throughout the month. This will not only help you to avoid disputes but also be essential to meeting your savings goals.

How to read/use a bank statement

It is important to keep up with and track your accounts on a weekly or bi-weekly schedule. It's also a good idea to keep a checkbook or account register of all the transactions you make over the week so you can reconcile everything with your bank, and make sure there are no unexpected transactions or fraud happening on your account. There is helpful software out there like Quickbooks or Quicken or a simple Excel document to help you achieve this. Or you can go old school and use a manual handwritten checkbook register to record all your spending transactions. Each type of financial institution will have its own way of displaying transactions on your account, but they all offer a similar approach to how they handle your money and how it is spent. Your bank statement will include how much money you started with – this is referred to as the starting balance – and any funds that were used throughout the period in question. You should check your statements often and reconcile your spending. If you don't, you could find your account in a mess that you have to spend days, weeks, or months cleaning up.

Chapter Three

Managing Your Money and Budget Building

S tatistics show that two-thirds of Americans don't have a budget, and over half have less than $1,000 in savings. What's worse is that those who do have a budget spend much more than they earn. If you are just beginning to learn about money management or you're looking for tips to budget better, then this is the guide for you! This chapter will help you learn about creating a monthly budget, building an emergency fund, and saving money. By the end, you'll have a solid foundation ready for the rest of your independence journey!

What is an emergency fund? What is a monthly budget? How do you save money? These are some of the questions that most people have at one point or another. I've created this guide to provide pointers and tips to help you get started down the right path!

Over the years, I have met and consulted many people who spend more than they make. In my younger years, I was just like everyone else, spending more than I was making. I have since learned that budgeting, managing bills wisely, paying off debt, and saving money is the key to having financial freedom and to living comfortably. It also will help you know when to say "No" to frivolous spending and take a break from purchasing things that don't matter. This chapter contains many tips on how you can save money and become financially independent.

What is a budget?

First off, let's quickly talk about what a budget is and why you need one. A budget is simply a list or plan for allocating funds for different bills, savings, investments, and personal desires. Your goal is to create less financial stress today to obtain your financial goals for tomorrow. So with my help, you will decide which budget buckets your income will be allocated.

If you want access to a fabulous budgeting workbook guide and working budget sheet you can use for yourself. You can download it here https://dadtothebone.com/budgetguide

One of the hard choices you have to make is where you want to budget your money. Which budget buckets do you allocate first and which ones do you not allocate if at all? It is a fact that some people like to spend their money as soon as they get it. If this is one of your habits and if you are deep in debt because of it, then I'm guessing budgeting is the right move for you.

The most difficult thing about budgeting is getting started. You must start somewhere, so pick a date to begin keeping track of your spending habits. My suggestion is to start immediately.

To begin, we first need to get a total of all your income and expenses when budgeting is done well, they should equal $0.00. I'm betting that if you're not budgeting properly, you'll either have a negative amount or a positive. But what we want is for your income and budget to be equal. This does not mean you will have $0.00 in the bank, it just means you know where every penny you have is budgeted.

As an example, let's consider Jane's income and expenses:

Jane has $2,200 per month in income and $3,145 per month in expenses. This leaves her with a deficit of $945 each month. How can Jane ever get ahead and not stress about how to make ends meet? Well, let's start by helping Jane make a budget and then figure out where Jane can cut costs and possibly bring in more income.

How to create a budget:

Step 1: List out all your current expenses and how much each cost and what date they're due. Think of each one as a bucket. Each bucket needs to be filled each month by the due date. These buckets should be broken up into three main categories of bills.

- **Foundational:** These are the bills that you must pay to survive. You need a roof over your head, warmth (electricity/gas), food (groceries), and water (utilities). These are the most important bills you want to make sure you have covered every month.

- **Niceties:** These are bills that if for some reason you could not or did not pay on time it wouldn't be the end of the world, or you can do without. Things like the Internet, cell phones (remember the world worked before cell phones were invented), and credit cards (you may get a late fee and more interest fees, but if you had to miss a payment it's not the end of the world), medical bills. You can sometimes work with the billing department and get on smaller payment plans or ask for a concession for a month.

- **Luxuries:** these are the non-essentials, but contribute to the quality of life (vacations, dining out, clothing purchases, etc.)

Your list of buckets should look something like this... of course, it will vary for your own personal situation.

Foundational:
Due: 1stRent ($1,000)
Due: 1stGroceries ($500)
Due: 15thElectric ($250)
Due: 15thWater ($30)

Niceties:
Due: 1stGas for Car ($480)
Due: 10thInsurance ($60)
Due: 25thCell Phone ($200)
Due: 25thInternet ($25)

Luxuries:
Due: 1stDining out ($400)
Due: 1st Clothing ($100)
Due: 1stVacation / Personal ($100)

Total Monthly Expenses: $3,145

What most people will find is they have more buckets and expenses than they have income. This is okay. This is all part of beginning to manage your finances and making some hard adult decisions on your spending so you can lower financial stress and create goals to create financial freedom.

Step 2: Write down your income buckets and the date you receive your income. List out all of the ways you bring money into your life, and make sure to include everything from regular income (such as a salary) to irregular income (from things like side hustles).

Using the example with Jane, it might look something like this...
Income:
Receive: 1st   Paycheck ($1,100)
Receive: 15th Paycheck ($1,100)

Total Monthly Income: $2,200

Step 3: Allocate funds. Many people will try to pay an entire bill with one paycheck, which in turn leaves them with very little or nothing at all right after their payday. Their bank accounts are always practically empty, and the possibility of having to use their overdraft protection and accruing more needless fees and expenses keeps them struggling to make ends meet. This can be avoided, and reduce this stress by allocating your money to budget buckets differently.

The first thing to do is organize your bills by date and then half the amount due for each bucket before you start allocating funds. What this basically means is to split your bills in half. Next, you will want to start filling the buckets in order 1. Foundational, 2. Niceties, then 3. Luxuries. If you run out of income before you make it to the end of your list, then you'll know which Niceties and/or Luxuries will need to be evaluated, if they are truly needed, or figure out a way to reduce the bill so you can afford it.

To ensure buckets are filled in time before the due date, Jane will need to use her 1st of the month paycheck and start filling in the buckets that are due on the 15th through the 31st. Once those buckets are filled, she will allocate the rest of the paycheck to the buckets that are for the 1st through the 15th. Then when she gets her paycheck on the 15th, she will first allocate money to the buckets from the 1st through the 15th, then allocate the rest of her paycheck from the 16th through the 31st.

In this example, Jane already has some buckets filled from her last paycheck which was on the 15th.

Type	Due Date	Bucket	Amount Filled
Foundational	1st	Rent ($1000)($500)	
Foundational	1st	Groceries ($500)($250)	
Niceties	1st	Gas for Car ($480)($240)	
Luxuries	1st	Clothing ($100)($50)	
Luxuries	1st	Dining out ($400)($200)	
Niceties	10th	Insurance ($60)($30)	$30
Foundational	15th	Electric ($250)($125)	$125
Foundational	15th	Water ($30)($15)	$15
Niceties	25th	Internet ($25)($13)	$13
Niceties	25th	Cell Phone ($200)($100)	$100
Luxuries	31st	Vaca/Personal ($100)($50)	$50

Now she just received her paycheck on the 1st for $1,100. She will start filling in all the Foundational buckets, first starting with the buckets 15th - 31st.

The Electric and Water only needed $140 from her $1,100 paycheck because the bucket was already half full from her previous paycheck. Now that those two foundational buckets are full, she will be able to pay the bill on time.

Type	Due Date	Bucket	Amount Filled
Foundational	1st	Rent ($1000)($500)	
Foundational	1st	Groceries ($500)($250)	
Niceties	1st	Gas for Car ($480)($240)	
Luxuries	1st	Clothing ($100)($50)	
Luxuries	1st	Dining out ($400)($200)	
Niceties	10th	Insurance ($60)($30)	$30
Foundational	15th	Electric ($250)($125)	**$250** ←
Foundational	15th	Water ($30)($15)	**$30** ←
Nicities	25th	Internet ($25)($13)	$13
Nicities	25th	Cell Phone ($200)($100)	$100
Luxuries	31st	Vaca/Personal ($100)($50)	

Now she has to allocate the rest of her $960 again, starting with the Foundational buckets first. After these two buckets are half full, Jane has $210 left to allocate. Jane has a choice of where she wants to allocate the remaining amount.

Type	Due Date	Bucket	Amount Filled
Foundational	1st	Rent ($1000)($500)	**$500** ⬅
Foundational	1st	Groceries ($500)($250)	**$250** ⬅
Niceties	1st	Gas for Car ($480)($240)	
Luxuries	1st	Clothing ($100)($50)	
Luxuries	1st	Dining out ($400)($200)	
Niceties	10th	Insurance ($60)($30)	$30
Foundational	15th	Electric ($250)($125)	$250
Foundational	15th	Water ($30)($15)	$30
Niceties	25th	Internet ($25)($13)	$13
Niceties	25th	Cell Phone ($200)($100)	$100
Luxuries	31st	Vaca/Personal ($100)($50)	

If Jane wanted to, she could reduce her grocery bill by making more casseroles and/or cheaper meals that can be made into leftovers. If this reduces the bill by $50, she can then fill the buckets for Internet and Insurance leaving her with $217 to allocate. If Jane can carpool with friends or take the bus if needed to reduce her gas for car bill to $150, she would have $67 to allocate to any of the other buckets she chooses. There are many ways to reduce expenses, like rent for example. Jane could find a roommate and lower her rent cost considerably, freeing up more income to allocate to other things.

Type	Due Date	Bucket	Amount Filled
Foundational	1st	Rent ($1000)($500)	$500
Foundational	1st	Groceries ($500)($250)	**$200** ⬅
Niceties	1st	Gas for Car ($480)($240)	**$150** ⬅
Luxuries	1st	Clothing ($100)($50)	
Luxuries	1st	Dining out ($400)($200)	
Niceties	10th	Insurance ($60)($30)	**$60** ⬅
Foundational	15th	Electric ($250)($125)	$250
Foundational	15th	Water ($30)($15)	$30
Niceties	25th	Internet ($25)($13)	**$25** ⬅
Niceties	25th	Cell Phone ($200)($100)	**$200** ⬅
Luxuries	31st	Vaca/Personal ($100)($50)	

What Jane accomplished by using her paychecks to pay only half a bucket at a time, allows her to keep money in the bank at all times. Even though these are all earmarked for other bills and expenses, she keeps all this money in the bank until the bill is actually paid. For example, the $500 for rent will be in her bank until the end of the month, which means if an emergency came up and she had to dip into any of these buckets, the money will be there; however, she'll have to remember there'll be more of the bucket to fill when the next paycheck comes.

So, what about all the buckets that didn't get filled? Well, this method allows you to decide how important all these buckets are to you. If you want to fill these buckets, but your current paycheck isn't getting you there, then the options are to get another job to bring in more income, start a side hustle to bring in more income, or find ways to reduce the current buckets freeing up more money to allocate to the other buckets. You might not be able to put in 100% of the amount you desire in your Niceties and Luxury buckets every month, but depending on how you reduce the amount due in your other buckets or add more income (bonuses, birthday money, etc.), you might find extra money to allocate at some point, then you just put it in the desired amount in those buckets and leave it there until you fill that bucket enough for you to spend it on the thing(s) you want. This is called making a goal and saving the amount you want to get the thing(s) you want.

Importance of budgeting

Sticking to a budget can be hard for many people. It forces you to be held accountable for your spending and savings. A budget can tell you, "No, you can not have that right now," and like a child, we don't like to be told "No" when we want something. Especially when it's your hard-earned money and you want to spend it the way you want. You can always spend your money as you please; however, when you go through tough financial times, you can't get mad when you don't have the money that you need when you need it due to poor planning and frivolous spending. Life will always throw you a curveball at some point. Don't be mad at the ball, you have to be mad at yourself for not being financially responsible. No one is going to do it for you, you have to do it yourself. Only you can decide what your financial position is going to be.

Some of the benefits to budgeting:

• You will save money.

• You will reduce the stress of financial problems.

• You will be able to realize and accomplish your goals and dreams.

• You might even get rich.

Budgeting is about controlling your spending and saving habits for you and your family.

More money doesn't mean more spending.

How often have you heard from a friend or relative who just came into some money that they're going to put it away in a nest egg or invest it for the future? How many of them actually do it? Not as many as you'd think. Most people who come into some money spend it right away. They convince themselves they deserve a reward, or they try to keep up with the Joneses, and they purchase things just to be able to say, "look at me and what I got." They go out and buy the new vehicles and clothes they've been craving. Some of them even go on shopping sprees and buy items they just don't need. Seventy percent of Lotto winners who've won $1 million or $500 million all lose or spend that money in five years or less. When you come into some extra money, the better plan would be to save some for an emergency or invest it to keep money coming in, and budget everything.

According to research, most Americans have less than $1,000 in savings. This is not much. The average household in America has over $10,000 in credit card debt alone. This is not good. If you have more than $1,000 in an emergency fund and no credit card debt, then you are already doing better than seventy-five percent of all Americans. If your emergency fund is less than $1,000 and your credit card debt is more than zero, then you will need to change how you handle money immediately if you want to improve your personal finances.

What is an emergency fund?

An emergency fund is just what it sounds like. It's a bucket of money put off to the side for emergency situations. It shouldn't be used for immediate expenses or paying off debts when there is an unexpected event that can't wait for a paycheck.

If you're living paycheck to paycheck, building an emergency fund will be one of the most challenging budget buckets to fill. I used to live with no emergency fund and no real budget. I was always stressed about what would happen if my car broke down, my water heater or dishwasher needed repair, what if I had to go to the doctor or get a tooth fixed. When I decided to start my emergency fund, I could only afford $10 to start. Whenever I could, I would add more to it. It took over a year to get it to $100 and it felt great to have $100 for an emergency. Then an emergency happens, and the emergency budget bucket was brought back to zero. I learned then to work harder at building a larger fund. And now, when I have any extra money I don't have a bucket for and I could spend it on crap, I put it into my emergency fund.

A well-managed emergency fund will give you peace of mind knowing that you can cover costs when an emergency happens and ensure that you don't have to turn elsewhere for the money—such as a loan from family or a high-interest credit card.

Getting financially stable is possible and can be easy to do. It takes planning, hard work, and perseverance on your part. However, if you follow these simple budgeting tips and tactics, your dreams and goals are achievable.

How much money do I need in an emergency fund?
Having a cash reserve will allow you to rest easily at night and know that money is available if something

goes wrong. There are many suggestions for how much money should be in an emergency fund. If you're struggling with your budget, then your first goal should be to get $100 into the emergency fund bucket. This might not seem like much, but when an emergency hits, it can make all the difference. But don't stop there. Keep adding and growing it, but do your best not to let it get below $100 for very long.

The average emergency is $400, and it can take up to six months to make a full recovery. That means that if you have $2,000 in an emergency fund, you can expect to use $400 of that money every six months. Even though this doesn't look like much, think about how your life would change if you had no money at all.

Dave Ramsey suggests putting yourself on a cash diet. He says to take the amount of money you spend every month (on average, 20 percent of it is squandered away on luxuries not niceties). Save that money - don't use it for anything else but saving. You should aim to save this 20 percent until you have two months of expenses set aside in your emergency fund. If you make only $3,000 a month, that means that you need to save $600 every month and put it in your savings account. These are easy goals, and even if you don't have an extra $600 to put away each month, there are other ways to make money even if it's for a short while.

The Dave Ramsey method

Dave Ramsey is not someone I heard about in my years starting out. As a matter of fact, he was just starting out to become the financial guru he is today. Dave Ramsey is one of the most well-known finance experts for personal finance strategies and advice. The Dave Ramsey method has seven parts:

1. Start an emergency fund - save $1,000 for emergencies.

2. Focus on your debts - Pay Off All Debt (Except the House). Dave Ramsey's debt reduction plan is to pay off small debts first, then work your way up to the bigger debts, like your car, credit cards, and student loans.

3. Complete your emergency fund - grow your emergency fund to be able to cover 3 to 6 months of expenses.

4. Save for Retirement - Invest 15% of Your Household Income in Retirement.

5. Save for College - If you can pay for your kid's college tuition, then you'll ensure their financial security in the future.

6. Pay off your house - Put all the extra monthly income you have into your mortgage so you can finish paying it off early.

7. Build Wealth - Start focusing on building your wealth.

Unfortunately, it was much later in life when I found Dave Ramsey and his strategies for financial freedom. I found that I could adapt and apply some of his ideas to what life decisions have been teaching me over the years to come up with a plan that worked for my budget and family to achieve the same goals.

Build an emergency fund the Dave Ramsey way

Dave Ramsey suggests that the best way to create an emergency fund is to set up a recurring automatic money transfer to a savings account. This money can be used for any expense, and you can't spend it before the time period has passed.

To create an automatic transfer of money in your checking account, do the following:

- Begin by ordering a paper checkbook and making two copies of your checkbook card. One copy goes into your wallet, the other goes into your safe deposit box if you own one.

- Throughout the week, write out a check for cash to deposit into your savings account.

- Fill out the check and record the amount in your

checkbook ledger.

- Deposit this check at the bank where you have your savings account.

- Once the new copies of your checks are paid out, go home and lock one copy in a safe deposit box or keep it in another secure location. Dave Ramsey encourages people to have a little bit of extra money every month as an emergency fund. It is important to put this money into a place where you can't get it.

The emergency fund you build should give you the ability to cover six to twelve months of expenses if you suddenly lose your job.

Chapter Four

Building Your Credit

When I was young, before I ever moved out of my parent's home to be on my own, my father once told me something I'll never forget. "Credit is one of the hardest things to obtain and the easiest to ruin," and it's so true. So, what is a credit score? How do you build your credit score? Credit scores can fluctuate depending on how much credit you have in use, how well you pay your bills on time, how much debt you've incurred, and how long you've had a credit history with a business.

What is a credit score? Why is it important?

Back in the day, you used to be able to go to a bank and have an honest conversation with a loan officer, work out a loan deal with them, and walk away with a pretty decent loan with a decent interest rate. Nowadays, banks don't care about your payment history or relationship with them. No matter how long you've been banking with them and how well you've paid on your loans, they review your credit score and make decisions from that number. A credit score is a three-digit number from 300 - 850 that you are given when you apply for any type of credit card, car loan, personal loan, or buying a home. It's intended to let lenders know how well you manage your credit, how new you are to having credit, how likely it is that you will pay your debts back, and what type of interest you will pay on a loan.

If your credit score is low, you could have higher interest rates when borrowing money. If it is too low, you may be declined a loan or credit cards altogether. A higher credit score gives you a better chance of getting a lower interest rate. This means it will save you money when you buy a car, motorcycle, home mortgage, or pay for your rent. Credit scores that range from 580 to 669 are considered pretty fair. The average credit score is around 698, 670 to 739 is considered good credit, and 740 to 799 is considered very good; 800 and up is considered having excellent credit.

But do not worry if you have a low score! You can build or rebuild your credit score even if you already have bad or insufficient credit! Your credit scores indicate how much risk there is to lend you money.

How do I start building my credit score?

To start building a credit score, you'll need to borrow money from some sort of lender that reports to the credit bureaus. This could be in the form of a car loan, a house loan, a personal bank loan, or a credit card. One way to start building credit is to take out a small $1,000 personal loan from your bank. You can use the money you borrow to pay the loan back gradually for a minimum of six months. This will help establish a payment history and how well you pay on time. Then you can use the tool CreditKarma.com which will help guide you on what is affecting you positively and negatively and how to understand and fix these issues.

Credit cards can be a great tool for people to develop a good credit score, but also have plenty of hidden costs and can put you in a mountain of debt very fast. The temptation of easy money is what gets people in trouble quickly if they are not responsible with their spending. You can request credit reports from your bank and the credit bureaus; however, CreditKarma.com will be able to give you what you need and is pretty close to being as up-to-date as a real credit report.

How do I get a higher credit score?

You want to make sure you're paying your bills on time at least 98% of the time if you want to have or maintain a high credit score. If you pay less than 98% on time, your credit score will suffer from this. How much revolving credit you have can also play a part in your score.

You want to try to only use up to 30% of your available credit. Once you go over 30% usage, your credit score could be affected. Two ways to have a reduced percentage is to either pay down your bills or raise the amount of available credit you have. If your credit and debt-to-income is good, you can either ask your credit company to raise your credit limit or open a new credit card with a good limit on it, but don't use the credit card. Remember, the goal is just to get more available credit than you are using.

Derogatory remarks on your credit report can lower your score very fast. A derogatory remark means you've not paid your bill, and your bill has been sent to a collection agency or court. Having just one derogatory remark can lower your score significantly, and a derogatory remark can stay on your credit history for up to 7 - 10 years. It's best to work and communicate with your collectors to work out payment plans should you struggle to pay your bills. They will usually work with you, but ignoring them and not paying your bill will only hurt you in the long run. This is how I learned what my father meant when he said it's easy to ruin your credit. The good news is it's salvageable and can be corrected, and you can still get a good credit score over time by being responsible with your finances.

Your credit history plays a factor in your score. There is no way to speed up this part of your score. The best you can do is start your credit history sooner rather than later so you have more time to have on record the way you manage your credit. You'll want a minimum of 5 - 6 years of credit history for it to start affecting your credit score positively. Seven to eight years is even better, but 9+ years is considered excellent history.

How many different credit accounts you have also play a part in your credit score. Just because you have credit accounts doesn't mean you have to use them. If you only have one credit account, one does not show a potential lender that you can manage more than one loan at a time. You will still be considered a risk even if you're paying your bills on time. For your score to start changing for the better, you'll want to obtain over ten different credit lending accounts. Eleven to twenty accounts is where you'll start seeing your score improve, but having over 21 accounts is where you'll obtain your best scores, as long as all 21 accounts are in good standing and not using more than 30% of your overall available credit.

One of the last things that play a factor in your credit score is hard inquiries. A hard inquiry means that a lending company has checked your credit score because you are working on obtaining a line of credit. Each time a bank, credit card company or lending company checks your credit, it shows on your credit report.

You want to try to keep your inquiries below four if possible. One or two inquiries or less is an optimal amount of inquiries. Inquiries can stay on your credit report for up to 2 years. The good news is it's a temporary ding and scores usually bounce back in 3 months. You'll want to plan ahead and minimize your hard inquiries for at least 9-12 months before trying to get a mortgage or big loan.

Credit reports

A credit report is what your history of credit looks like. It shows you how much money you owe and to whom. It also shows how much outstanding debt you have, how well you paid on your loans, if they were paid on time or if they are in default. It will show how many times you've applied for a loan and credit which can hurt your score, and it will show if you have any debt turned over to debt collectors, which also hurts your credit score.

FICO (Fair Isaac Corporation) maintains three consumer credit files — a commercial file, a retail file and a mortgage loan file — on virtually every consumer in the United States who has borrowed any type of money, including credit cards, car loans and mortgages.

Therefore, it's important to pay them all off eventually because everything impacts your score in one way or another. Obviously, it's harder to get approved when you have a lot of outstanding debt. So, if you want to start building your credit, pay off any debts you may have first. If you currently have any type of credit, it's important to make sure you make your payments on time.

Good debt vs. bad debt

When it comes to money, some people don't see the difference between good debt and bad debt. This is why I want to define them for you in terms of what they are and what they mean. Good debt can be defined as something that will help you build your credit history or help you out financially, such as a car loan or student loan. Bad debt will only hurt you and make it harder for you to borrow more money, like credit card debts and personal loans.

Bad debt should be paid off as soon as possible, so you won't have to pay extra interest. Paying off these additional charges will make credit less complicated for you because the smaller the outstanding debts the better.

Everyone has to start somewhere, so if you have the chance to get a loan or financing for any type of purchase – go for it! If you can afford it, then do it. Use the money for something that will help build your credit and ensure that your payments are on time each month so that your balance gets smaller and smaller each month.

Another thing to remember is not to apply for many loans all at once, which would hurt your score instead of helping it.

Debt consolidation vs. refinancing

If you have multiple debts accrued from different sources, you have a great chance of negatively impacting your FICO score by paying off one of them quickly and causing the others to fall behind schedule. Therefore, it's important to consolidate or refinance all your debts in order to pay them off together and lower your interest payments in the long run.

If you have multiple debts with interest rates over 10% or 15%, it makes sense to refinance those bad debts into one new loan. Instead of having $1,000 getting 10% interest paying $100 a month, and another debt of $2,500 paying 18% interest also paying over $100 a month, you can try to consolidate these into one payment with one smaller interest rate; $3,500 at 9% interest with one bill to pay $100 a month. Now you just reduced your monthly expenses by $100. Not only can this help you sometimes save hundreds of dollars a month, but it will also give you one easy monthly payment instead of five or more individual ones. Just be careful of the temptation of having extra money to start spending again. That extra money should be used to re-budget it for something important or help pay off debt faster.

Do your homework and the math to make sure you're getting the best consolidation deal at the best interest rate. You may find that it's more advantageous only to consolidate two of your three bills. Maybe one bill has a good interest rate and is almost paid off. You can consolidate two bills and save some money to make a larger payment to the third bill, paying it off early, thus getting yourself that much further out of debt faster.

What is a line of credit?

A personal line of credit is an open-ended loan that allows you to withdraw funds as needed for a set period of time. Personal lines of credit can be issued for limits ranging from $1,000 to over $100,000, and you will not be able to exceed this amount.

Interest begins accruing immediately once funds are withdrawn; interest is only charged on the outstanding balance until it's paid off during a preset repayment schedule. You will want to make minimum monthly payments similar to a credit card. The minimum re-payment amount varies but can be charged as a fixed fee or percentage of the balance owed, usually 1% or $25—whichever is higher.

A line of credit is a bank loan that you can use to cover any money shortages you may have during the month. Most people don't use lines of credit as often as they should because they're usually too nervous about how much it will cost them, but this is not the case at all! In fact, lines of credit are straightforward to obtain and can be beneficial in many ways.

Pros of having a line of credit

- Borrow only the money you need

- Interest incurred only on funds borrowed

- Flexible repayment options

- Constant access to funds

- Lower average APR than credit cards

- Unsecured credit lines risk no collateral

- Option to provide collateral for lower interest rates (secured loan)

- Few restrictions on the use

- Ideal for long-term projects where the final costs are variable

- Ideal for meeting temporary cash shortfalls

- May draw up to 100% of credit limit without restrictions

Cons of having a line of credit

- Non-deductible interest expense

- If interest rates increase, the variable rate on the line of credit also increases

- Annual/monthly maintenance fees, regardless of use

- Higher rates than fixed-rate loans; not ideal for debt consolidation

- The amount of interest charged may be more difficult to forecast

- Fees/APRs vary widely by provider

- Usually requires an account at a lending institution

- Requires a good credit score to qualify

- Poor solution for long-term cash shortfalls

- The temptation to spend due to ease of access

- Persistently high balance can decrease credit score

The decision to move out of your family's home, or if you are a parent trying to help your child move out of the house, is a big deal. I moved out at a very young age. As well, I have successfully launched two of my four children out into the real world so far, helping them spread their wings and leave the nest. There are a lot of things that have to be considered and planned for to have the smoothest transition possible.

Chapter Five

Moving Out Guide

Are you ready to move out?

Moving out can be one of the best, most exciting, stressful decisions one can make. Before making this decision, there are some important questions you first need to ask yourself. These questions will help you know if moving out is something you want or need to do. The decision to move out may be based more on a desire to leave your parents' house than your ability to support yourself. Moving out is a big decision that should not be taken lightly, so take the time to make sure you have everything you need before you move out.

1. How much money do I have saved up? How much debt do I have? How much debt will I have? The first step in your moving-out process is to assess how financially stable you are. This will help determine if you can afford to live on your own and what kind of living arrangement would be right for you.

2. Do I have a job? How are you going to support yourself and pay your bills? Do you have a solid plan to get your finances together before taking the leap of faith to move out?

3. Am I ready financially? You will have more financial obligations as an adult than when you were living at home. If you are currently living on your parent's dime, this can be very beneficial in getting your financial foundation built. Build good habits now so you'll struggle less when you're free and independent.

4. Am I ready emotionally? Moving out of your childhood home is a huge step. This new independence can make you feel overwhelmed and excited at the same time. It's okay to be nervous or scared. Don't forget, this is hard on your parents, too, to see their child they've loved, watched over, and nurtured not needing them any longer.

5. Do I have good credit? The decision to move out often means you will finally be free from your parent's eyes. This means that they're not going to be around to see the step you're about to take, a step you're not fully prepared for, and try to lunge out to grab you before you hurt yourself like when you were a toddler. It's not up to your parents to choose how many credit cards or loans you have or how you spend your money. It is still very important that you learn to maintain a good credit score so you can obtain cars and houses when you need them. According to the credit reference bureau, the data from Experian shows that 16% of Americans (48 million people) have poor credit. Let's work together not to have you be one of those 48 million people.

6. What about school? If you are currently going to a university, high school, or trade school, you will want to put more thought into your decision to move out. It might be more beneficial to work out a situation with your parents to allow you to stay at home a little longer than you desire while you work on building your financial foundation. The reason for this is to have the safety net of your parents while you learn to be independent. But you have to work at being independent and respect your parents' house and rules. Work out a moving-out plan with them. Start taking on more of your own financial responsibilities while you're still at your parent's home. Start taking care of their house as if it was your own; do your own laundry, dishes, yard work, etc. Get a real feel of what it will be like to be on your own and independent. Your parents will more than likely appreciate your added help and even feel more confident that you're ready to leave the nest.

7. Am I ready to be independent? As hard as it may be, moving to adult living will be one of the most important steps in your life, and you need to face it head-on.

Switch Your Bills to Your Name

One of the first things you need to do if you are going to become independent is to put bills into your own name so that all your bills and loans go to you and not your parents. This is very important because as an adult, you will need to have money and budget accordingly instead of pulling every dime out of your mom's purse or dad's wallet. Most banks, credit card companies, and phone companies will allow you to do this transfer on-line or over the phone with a simple request. This will not only help you gain financial independence, but also allow you to keep an eye on your own accounts, which will make managing your money easy.

Where are you going to live?

Finding a home is a very exciting and sometimes a stressful experience. You're probably going to be eager to get started. You might have even found the perfect place with the right amount of space and floor plan you love. You'll more than likely be there for a long time, so what about the area where this home is located? Are you looking for a place with a certain school access, a certain distance from work or your family, or where there is a good nightlife? The kind of area you desire matters because once you're in it, you may have to be in it for a long time and you don't want to be in a place where you're not happy. Deciding where you are going to live will help you decide if moving out of your parent's home is the best move for your situation at this time. Be patient and find the right place for you.

Factors to consider
There are many factors that need to be considered when choosing the best place to live. Here are some of the key questions that you should consider:

1. What is the average cost of rent? Housing costs vary greatly from one part of the country to another and from one area to another within the same city. The best way to find good deals on housing and rent at a reasonable price is to use a housing website like Zillow.com or Realty.com to look up rental and housing costs in areas near you, or you can contact people that already live in this area.

2. How close does it feel to work? A long commute can get draining after a long time. Knowing the traffic situation should be a factor. Choosing a home located close enough for you not to be bothered getting up in the morning, driving long distances, using up a lot of gas, and fighting traffic can make all the difference between a good or bad day. You'll have to weigh out the pros and cons of your home's location. Don't be in a rush when home hunting. Keep looking for that perfect home that has the perfect distance you desire. It's out there. You just have to keep looking for what's right for you.

3. Is it safe? There are many areas that are starting to become dangerous, and your safety is important as far as where you decide to live. Choosing the right place to live is one of the most important things in moving out.

4. Are there a lot of things to do? This is one of the reasons that many people prefer smaller towns over bigger cities. The fewer people you have in your town, the less chance there will be of trouble brewing.

5. Does it have good schools? If you are going to be living at home when you finish school, this is one of the most important factors to consider. You need to make sure that if you have children, that they will be able to attend a good school.

6. How close is it to family? This can be a very important factor if you are going to be living at home while finishing school or in the area while working. Being close enough that your family or friends can come over and see you won't matter if they can't afford it on their own.

7. How old is the area? Many areas are taking steps to make sure that older residents are cared for in their communities, and some areas offer discounts on rent if you move in before a certain date.

8. Do people know each other? This can be very important as an adult because while living at home, it is a good idea to have many friends around you or have a large circle of friends so that people can help with things like driving you places, helping you get around, or just being there for you if you need them.

Income requirements
Making sure you can pay your bills but still have some extra money in the bank can be very important in deciding where you will live. If you are living at home, this means that you might want to find ways to save money and make sure it is put away each month before you fly from the nest.

Here are some things to consider when making this decision:

Do you need a roommate?
Roommates can mean a lot of money in your pocket as far as saving money. A roommate can help split the cost of rent, utilities and food. Having a roommate can also help make a place feel less lonely at times. However, roommates can also have its challenges if living habits conflict.

How much are you paying for rent?
If you are trying to save money or you're on a fixed income (i.e.: Medicaid, food stamps or Section 8), it may be necessary for you to try and find places where the rent is not so high that it will cause problems for you in the long run.

How much will you pay for utilities?

This can be very important as far as finding a place to live. The less you spend on utilities, the more money you will have in your pocket to save or put away. Some places have some utilities included in the rent. Shop for the best place with the best deal for your budget.

What is the average rent around there?

Use realty websites to research the pricing of houses and rentals to make sure you're getting the best deal and not overpaying in rent.

Can you afford to pay utilities?

This can be very helpful in deciding where you will live. You can ask landlords in the area or question realtors who are selling houses in the area about what the average utilities cost.

Does your landlord have good reviews?

This is not a factor that is usually listed in the newspaper, but it is something that should be looked at when you are looking for a place to live. A bad landlord can make life very difficult for you and there are some good landlords out there as well, so finding a landlord that will help you with repair issues or offer discounts on rent can be helpful.

What to do if you don't have enough to move out

If you find yourself in a situation where you are unable to move out, there are steps that can be taken in order to help your situation. The first thing to do is set up a budget. This will allow you to see where your money is going every month, as well as help you see where you can save. Saving money can be done by getting a second job, cutting back on expenses, or even having a garage sale and selling some of your belongings. There are many things that should be considered when making sure that you have enough money to move out, and the best place to start is by looking at your budget and seeing what can be done.

Setting up a budget
As mentioned in Chapter 3, making sure that you have a good idea of what you are spending your money on each month can be one of the best things to do when trying to save money. You should consider your basic expenses like rent, food and gas, as well as things like clothes, entertainment and hobbies. Getting an idea of how much these things cost each month will help you see where you can cut back or where it is okay to spend more money. This will also allow you to see if there are places where you could make repairs or change things around for it not to eat up so much of your monthly income.

Cut back on stuff
One of the hardest adult things to do is cut back on things you want but don't need. One quick way to start

having more income is to start cutting back on some of the expenses in your life. This can include things like cell phone plans, cable subscriptions, and subscriptions for internet TV services. Having a budget set up will help guide you in what to cut back on, but if there is something that you have a hard time letting go of, there are many places where people offer free stuff around town.

Start looking for a second job
A lot of people can find themselves in a situation where they are unable to move out and sadly, there doesn't seem to be any light at the end of the tunnel. This can happen very easily, and the things that you need to do in order to fix this issue will depend on what you are looking for. If you are willing to work a few extra hours a week or even some evenings and weekends, you can sometimes find space in your schedule where you can earn a bit more. This will help make money and allow you to live on your own without having anyone else help out.

Get help from family or friends
Another option to help you out with getting out of the situation that you are finding yourself in is to ask for help from others. This doesn't mean that you should necessarily go asking friends or family for money, but rather there are many people who have a little extra space where you can stay. This is also helpful if you

need to save up for an apartment because it will allow you to live somewhere until your place is ready.

Look into public housing
If everything else fails and you don't seem to be able to get yourself out of the situation that you are in, the next step that can be taken would be looking into public housing. There are many situations where people that are living paycheck to paycheck, or people with a low income, can find themselves in a situation where it doesn't seem like they will ever be able to make enough money in order to move out. There are many places that offer help for those who need it.

Apply for assistance
There are also places around town where assistance can be given for housing if you find yourself in a situation where it doesn't seem like you will ever be able to get out. Some of these places include the Housing Choice Voucher program and Section 8 housing. These both offer some form of public housing or subsidized housing for those who qualify, and most of the time this is based on income levels.

Tips for choosing a roommate

Another aspect of moving out is finding a roommate. This is always a great way to save money, but it can be a little bit difficult when you are trying to find someone with whom you can share your living area. There are many things that should be considered before moving in with someone else that will make the process easier.

Get to know your roommate before moving in
This is something that many people seem to skip on, but is extremely important. It is important to make sure that you get to know someone before bringing them into your home, and it is also important that you build trust with them as well. Living together can be a great way to save money, but it can also be a very stressful and difficult situation if you are not sure what you are getting into.

Talk about finances
You should discuss finances with the person that you are thinking about moving in with you. You should have a firm understanding of what the person can and cannot do financially, and also make it a point to tell them your financial situation. This will let you both know what you are getting into, and it will help avoid any future problems.

Discuss responsibilities
There are some people out there who want to live by themselves, while others don't mind living with other people. It is important that everyone makes it clear what they expect from the other person when it comes to financial contributions and keeping up with certain household responsibilities. This will help make sure that everyone is on the same page. Get things in writing

so nobody is going off memory months later which can cause arguments. Having things written down allows you to go to the agreement you both had when you started.

Be open and honest
It is also important that you are honest with the person that is moving in with you. This is a roommate, not a spouse, so sometimes it is better just to be upfront about things rather than trying to hide it. If you keep things like this a secret and end up getting further into the problem, it can make it worse or even cause problems in your relationship.

The steps above have been presented to help make the process move along and easy for those who need to find a roommate. The point of this is not to make it seem like this is an easy process and that everyone should just move out and find their own place, but the reality is that there are many people out there who need additional roommates or want a place to live.

Sharing an apartment

Sharing an apartment can be a great way to save money, and it is often the only option for some people. There are many ways to do this and save some money, but it can be difficult because there are so many variables that play into making this work. For example, if there are two people living in a one-bedroom apartment, then usually it will just become a matter of who sleeps where and how much space is left over during the day

How much space is there?
The apartment does not have to be big and it does not have to be cramped, but it does need to have enough room for each person to have their own space whenever they want or need it. Either way, someone is going a little bit under budget when they decide to share an apartment, and this can cause disagreements between roommates which will lead to arguments over nothing.

Who pays what?
This is one of the most important parts of agreeing to live with someone else, and it can be difficult at times. Each person needs to know what their financial responsibilities are and also have a clear understanding of how much each person should pay. Often there is more than one roommate, and then people assume that the others will just chip in when they can or if they do not have to work. Get it in writing so you can confirm you both agree and it can be referenced at any time.

What chores?
Everyone has different standards when it comes to cleaning up, etc., but it is important that everyone knows what they need to do and when they need to do it. This will help keep things running smoothly, especially if there are two people in the house.

What else?
There are always things that come up in these situations, and the important thing is to make sure that you are both aware of what the other person needs to do. This should be considered when moving in together and will help avoid problems down the line. The last thing that you want is a roommate who lives in your place and never contributes or cleans up after themselves.

Talk about expectations
It is also very important to discuss expectations with the person that you are moving in with. You want to make sure you understand their pet peeves and you can express yours to work out compromises for a healthy living situation without ending up getting on each other's nerves.

Rental insurance

Rental insurance is something that a lot of people forget to get, but it can be an important thing to have. Renters' insurance is also known as tenants' insurance. When you rent a house or an apartment, you don't want to find yourself in a position where you have to pay out of pocket for liabilities. Tenant Insurance helps protect tenants against such things as theft, property damage due to break-ins or a visitor's injury, or other perils.

Rental insurance covers what you own, whereas your landlord's insurance only covers the building and appliances they've purchased. The things you own can add up to more than you realize. The average person has over $35,000 worth of belongings.

There are three common types of insurance – personal property, liability, and additional living expenses. Personal property insurance covers your things that might get damaged or destroyed unexpectedly like floods or fires. It can help replace furniture and clothes, for example. Liability helps cover medical expenses or damage to other people's things or if your dog bites someone. You don't want to have to pay out of your savings for such an expense.

Do I need Coverage
Renters' insurance is important to have but not required. You should take a moment to approximate your possessions and think about if they were all lost in a fire. Would you like to replace them yourself or have an insurance company do it for you? This is something that you need to figure out for yourself and your budget because life has many ways to throw you curveballs. How prepared will you be if an unfortunate event happened? How much impact will it have on your savings if you don't have it? Here are some things to think about when you're deciding if you should get renters insurance.

The biggest reason why anyone should consider insurance is that you just never know what could be in store for you down the road. Whether this is a minor problem like a broken window or something more major like an electrical fire, you do not want to have to pay for these types of problems yourself.

Another reason why you should consider renters insurance is because it is affordable. Many people think that they cannot afford it and that they would never need it, but this is simply not the case. If you look around a little bit, then you can usually find a policy for $20 or less per month, which means that having the coverage will come at a very low cost for most people and that it will be affordable for most budgets.

Choose the Right Coverage Amount
While every insurance company is different, you should be careful to choose the right amount of coverage. Many people think that they are better protected by finding insurance for a few hundred dollars to get the maximum amount of coverage so that they don't have to pay too much out of pocket. This might be true in some cases, but it can get more expensive than you initially thought.

For instance, if a fire causes $1,500 in damages to your personal property and your deductible is $500, then your insurer will pay you $1,000. Your tenant insurance premiums will reflect the deductibles you agree to pay.

Lower deductibles mean higher premiums; higher deductibles mean lower premiums.

When you're just starting out, you should, at a minimum, consider something like $100,000 of personal liability coverage. This should be just enough coverage to cover the value of your personal property.

Understand the Different Coverage Types
Renters' insurance can be broken down into different types, and it can come in several different forms as well. Each type of coverage that you can get will also have a different deductible amount. In fact, there are many different types of deductibles, and it is important to know exactly what you will be paying for each one so that you do not end up paying as much out of pocket.

There are two very clear selections when it comes to renters insurance. There is liability coverage, which is the most common type of policy, and then there is medical coverage. It is usually called Med Pay in some parts of the country. The two of these are commonly combined, but they each have their own distinct purpose.

Liability coverage is there to protect you if anyone gets hurt in your home or apartment. Many people don't think someone will get hurt in their home and don't think that someone might come after them for medical expenses or more. If someone was to get hurt under your roof, a lawsuit could be brought against you, and it could result in very costly legal and medical fees.

This type of coverage will cover the cost of any medical bills that result from an injury that happens anywhere in a house or apartment. Tons of people think that this type of coverage is necessary because it does not sound like a lot at all, but you will soon be surprised at how much these claims can end up costing.

While this type of coverage is important and will cover the costs of any medical bills, it will not cover all of them. For instance, if someone does not have any medical coverage and ends up with a serious injury because they did not have proper insurance, then it is likely that you are going to be responsible for the full cost of their bills.

The main difference between the two types of coverage is a liability claim happens when the accident is the renter's fault. A medical payment claim is when someone hurts themselves, but it wasn't the renter's fault. In the end, when you cause a problem or accident, you will likely have to pay for it.

Pitfalls and traps with Renting.

Underestimating the cost
Moving out is an expensive exercise. Rental prices have soared in recent years. Even if you carefully budgeted

for rent and bills, things could still come up that may be unexpected. The cost of moving out will vary according to the length of a tenancy and the condition of the property at the end of the tenancy. There are many little things that can add up and cause hidden costs when moving from one place to another.

Ask about utilities
This is a question that should always be asked first because it will probably be the main thing that you need to decide on. Utilities are usually a monthly charge on the rent that goes to the landlord. This can include gas, water, trash, and electricity services.

When you are looking for an apartment or house, whether online or in person, ask the landlord if they have a utility company that owns and maintains the property. This is important because if you need something repaired or fixed, your landlord will have to send out a technician to fix any problems rather than him coming over and doing it himself or herself. If you're looking at a place that has its own energy provider, make sure they are reliable.

Having an idea of what utilities are included in the rent can be helpful as well. For instance, not all areas have cable TV and internet service, so be sure to inquire about both. If you know what things are covered by you and which by the landlord, then have the conversation upfront. You will know how much of your rent money goes toward these things.

Normally, it's the landlord's responsibility to fix utility issues, and it normally doesn't come out of the pocket of the renter unless something is at fault by the renter. Sometimes landlords don't want you messing with appliances and utilities without their permission. You do not want to make the owner upset or start charging you for things you touched and weren't supposed to.

Read the lease
Before you even think about getting any type of policy, you need to read your lease and find out what it says about any coverage that your landlord has on their end. You want to make sure that you are not paying for something that will be covered by them instead of yourself. If the landlord has insurance or any other kind of protection, they should tell you in the lease when they do, and then they should also be responsible for taking care of it.

Look at the apartment before moving
If you are planning on moving, then you may want to take a look at the apartment that you are moving into first. This is something that you should do even if it is just by looking from the outside and seeing how things line up. If there are any issues with the apartment, then point them out and discuss it with the landlord before ever signing a contract and moving in. If something

needs to be fixed, make sure there is a provision in the contract stating the landlord will fix it in a timely manner.

Chapter Six

Guide To Home Living on A Budget

When you first get out on your own for the first time, you might feel the need to fill the home with all the cool stuff. You think about the lifestyle you've had growing up and that your parents have provided for you over the years. Big screen TVs, computers, LED lighting, a kitchen with a full dining set and utensils, a nice large sofa, and an entertainment system.

When you want to invite people to come over, you want them to be impressed. You want to give the appearance that you've got it all figured out and are living large. I've seen many people want to impress others so much they put themselves in serious debt rather than live within their means and what they can really afford. It's okay not to have the best or biggest television, you don't have to have all the best dinnerware, a large dining table, the huge couch to watch the game with all your friends, or a fancy car to drive.

One of my favorite sayings from the movie "Fight Club" with Brad Pitt and Edward Norton. Brad Pit tells Edward's character, "We are consumers and byproducts of lifestyle obsession; the things you own can end up owning you." This is scary to think about; that you can put yourself in so much debt you work your butt off just to pay the bills on the things you own. Believe me, the things you want will come over time, but you need to be mentally strong to fight your wants over your needs. With the economy being fragile at best, it's essential to know how to live on a budget.

Wants vs. needs

How can you tell if something is a want or a need? You have to ask yourself when you're considering a purchase, "Is this something I need to have to survive?" "Can I do without it?" "Have I lived without it all this time up to this point?" If you can answer these questions honestly, nine times out of ten you can figure out if it goes in your want pile or your need pile. A need is something that if you don't have it, you're going to struggle until you have it.

Have you ever been online and are shown an ad for something cool, like a voice-controlled robot companion that will keep your schedule, take your messages,

and watch your house while you're gone? It's so perfect, right? You start thinking to yourself, "Man, that
would really be handy." You start thinking (justifying)
how this gadget will make your life SO much better.
When this starts to happen, I call this getting a monkey
on your back. This monkey is excited. It's working on
convincing you to spend the money and get the gadget.
If you're not careful and don't get rid of this monkey
on your back by being financially responsible to your
needs vs. wants, it will turn into a gorilla. A gorilla is so
much stronger and will tackle you into making the purchase. Before you know it, you make the unnecessary
purchases and the gorilla beats its chest and roars over
you because it won the purchasing wrestling match.

Many times after the purchase is made, you feel regret.
This is called buyer's remorse. When you realize you
didn't really need that thing and probably could have
used the money in a more strategic way, you might still
justify the purchase and maybe even hate that you did it
if you come up short for important expenses for which
you now don't have the money. Don't let monkeys stay
on your back for too long, and watch out for the gorillas.
Many of us spend too much money on things we know
we don't need. Therefore, it's important to think about
what you want to improve in your home and what you
need to survive in your home.

There are basics that everyone needs in their home, but
these should be the bare minimum, the foundational

stuff to make living easy and comfortable. Things like a working bathroom, a fully functioning kitchen, a bed to sleep in, etc. These are all items that make life livable, so make sure they're the focus of your needs first. Let's look at the basic areas around your home.

Essentials for the kitchen

Every home probably has a kitchen. In the kitchen should be a stove, sink, refrigerator, and freezer. Even if you aren't planning on making a meal every night, you should still have the essentials that can help you cook. Let's discuss some of the essential things you'll need for your kitchen when you're just starting out.

Cutlery and dishes: Since you will probably be eating often, you should have some spoons, knives, forks, plates, and bowls on hand. These are needed for cooking and eating. If you really want to save on your budget, you can start off with plastic ware that can be washed and reused. Over time, you can purchase the flatware and dishes you desire, purchase them over time, and build your collection.

Plasticware: It's a good idea to have some containers so that you can store leftovers. You will find when you're budget building, making large amounts of something to store and reheat is a great time and money savings tip anyone can accomplish.

Pots and pans: You should have at least two of each, a small and a large frying pan, a small and large cooking pot, a baking sheet, and maybe a roasting pan. This way, you can cook things separately. Don't buy something with too many parts or more than you need. Learn what you need before you start filling your kitchen with things you thought you would need and then never use. Spend wisely and keep it simple.

Trash: No one is going to pick up after you any longer. No one is going to tell you to take out the trash. This is your home now. If you don't take out the trash, then your home begins to turn into and smell like a dump. You'll need a 13 to 15-gallon trash can so it's big enough to hold everything you put in it, but not so big that you don't have to take it out often before it starts smelling. Also if it's too big, it won't fit in a discreet place.

Essentials for the bathroom

This is one place that we all visit every day, several times a day, and can easily become a host to bacteria or viruses. It's important that you keep it clean and tidy on a regular basis.

Towels: It is a good idea to have about five to six towels, bath-size as well as hand towels. This way you will not have to do laundry every day just to have a clean towel to dry yourself. You don't need a towel rack in your bathroom, but having one is a good idea. It will allow

116

you to keep all your towels fresh and dust-free, and it's also useful for allowing a towel to air dry. Tossing a wet towel on the floor or in a corner is a perfect way to create mildew and a smelly home.

Bar soap, shampoo and conditioner: Personal hygiene is important for healthy living habits. Having shampoo and conditioner to keep your hair healthy and your body clean is definitely an essential. You can consider buying these in bulk sizes to save on the cost of replenishing these items regularly.

Toothbrush and toothpaste: As you should be well aware, it's recommended you brush your teeth every day. It's always healthy living to keep your breath fresh and cavities away to avoid costly dentist bills.

Shaving cream and razor: This is something people forget about having around until you need it. If you really want to save a lot of money on shaving supplies, then I recommend purchasing one of those single-bladed razors where you can change out the blade. These razors cost less than $40 and last for many years. A pack of 200 blades costs about $15, and these blades can last you over a year, depending on how much shaving you do. Whereas, the more commercial razor heads with fixed blades that are made for a specific handle and are not very interchangeable can cost around $50 for 12 replacement heads and last less than three to six months.

Deodorant: Let's face it, we all sweat, and we all can have B.O. This investment is just part of life, and your friends will appreciate you having and using it. Having this in your home can help keep you odor-free all the time and make sure that your sweat stink doesn't smell too bad when you have to work hard during days or nights.

Toilet paper and feminine products: This may seem like a strange thing to mention here, but you can't just wipe with your hands, or I wouldn't recommend it anyway. If you're a woman, then you should know what you need and when you need it. This investment is just part of life, and you can't get away from having to purchase it and keep it stocked. Buying in bulk is a good idea because these products never go bad.

Essentials for the bedroom

A good night's sleep is very important for your mental health, productivity, and overall daily demeanor. If you want to feel good in your own home, then it's important to have a comfortable bedroom. This room is where you should be able to relax and get some sleep after a long day at work or school, so it's only fair that you set it up the way you want.

Bed: This is one of the most important things in your room since it will be where you spend most of your time when you're sleeping or just relaxing. When you're shopping for a bed, find out what kind of return policy the store or company has. Many times, trying out a mattress in the store doesn't give you a good feel for what it will be like after a full night's rest or even sleeping on the mattress for a week. Many stores and even some online mattress companies let you try the mattress for 90 days. These types of return options are a better deal so you can find what's best for you. Just be careful that some mattresses and frames can be very expensive, so make sure you're trying to stay within your budget while still getting a pain-free good night's sleep.

Pillows: You need to have pillows if you're going to have a nice night's sleep in your room. You can have many pillows if you like and always change them out if they start looking dirty or getting dust on them.

Sheets and pillowcases: You need to have sheets on your bed at the very least. Sheets and pillowcases protect your mattress and pillows, making them last longer from your body's sweat and dirt. You can get away with having one full set of sheets, but if you can at some point buy two full sets. That way, you can have a clean one on your bed while you're washing the other, keeping your bedding fresh all the time.

Blankets: While in the summer, blankets can be used as decorative pieces on your bed, during the winter they are used to keep you warm. However, make sure that when you store them away, they are clean and in good condition so they will be ready to use when winter comes again. Having too many blankets can also lead to a stuffy, humid room which makes it difficult to maintain comfortable temperatures on hot summer nights.

Alarm clock: This is a good way to wake up in the morning and get ready for the day. Choose one that has a radio or MP3 clock so it is easy to listen to your favorite music, programming, or news at exactly the time you want it.

Curtains: Curtains are used to block the sun from lighting up the room at night and also to keep the room temperature regulated throughout the night, depending on your goal for how much light you're trying to keep out of your room. Some curtains are made to keep all light out or just some. Choose what's best for your sleeping habits.

Keeping things Clean and Tidy

When you're just starting out, more than likely you won't have a lot of expendable cash. You want to save as much money as you can when you can. It's important to make sure you do your best to maintain, organize and clean your home. You are the only one who can hold yourself accountable for doing this work. Overwhelming chores and a messy house can become depressing and demotivating. You need to maintain your mental health, and part of your happiness and positive mental health is to have a clean, organized home. You need to be sure not to let things get out of hand because then the work piles up to become even more work.

I have some helpful tips to get you off to a solid start using some very easy DIY techniques that are easy and pocketbook-friendly.

DIY Cleaning Products
When it comes to cleaning your home, it's important to put safety first, so make sure you take steps to safeguard your DIY products by storing them properly as they will help you keep your home safe and clean as possible. Using DIY products can be budget friendly, but it's also important to know what you are doing. Here are some of the best DIY home cleaning products that you can use for your home.

Toilet Bowl Cleaner: Mix ¼ cup of Borax with 1 gallon of water in a bucket until it dissolves. Pour this solution into the toilet bowl and let it sit for 5-10 minutes before scrubbing clean. This will break down stains and deodorize the bowl at the same time.

Window Cleaner: Mix equal parts water and vinegar in a spray bottle and shake it up to mix well. Spray on the windows to give it a streak-free shine and wipe off with a clean cloth. These cleaning products are just as good as some commercial cleaners, if not better, but will cost you less money.

All-Purpose Cleaner: Mix ¼ cup lemon juice with 1 gallon of water in a bucket, then pour into a spray bottle. Spray onto your countertops, sinks and furniture, and wipe clean with a soft cloth. If you want to deodorize at the same time, add 10 drops of tea tree oil per gallon of water instead of the lemon juice.

Natural Stain Remover: Vinegar is an excellent natural stain remover. Just pour it directly onto the stain and scrub it with a soft brush or sponge. It can help break down stains such as wine, ink, coffee and tea. If you are worried about color bleeding into other fabrics, you can spray the vinegar onto a cloth before applying the cleaner to the whole surface. It's best to try a small area before doing the entire area to make 100% sure it doesn't damage the original surface.

Air Freshener: All you need is one small bowl or glass of 3 parts water to 2 parts lemon oil or extract to give your house a refreshing smell. You can even put a small bowl at each end of your home and in the bathroom for a real fresh scent that will last throughout the day.

The easiest option ever is to make your own dried citrus! It's very simple. Slice a bunch of lemons, limes, or oranges thinly. Bake them in the oven at 200 degrees for 3-4 hours until they're dried. Now you can place them wherever you'd like to freshen up. Your home will smell fantastic when you're baking them. The dried pieces can be ground up into potpourri and even re-used by boiling a small pot of water with the dried fruit chunks for a refresher fragrance in the house. You can even put it inside your closets. Win-win!

Liquid Laundry Detergent:

INGREDIENTS

1 cup Borax

1 cup washing soda

1 cup Castile soap (I use the lavender scent)

10-15 drops of essential oil (optional)

17 cups water

INSTRUCTIONS

1. In a large saucepan, bring 6 cups of water to a slight boil. Once the water begins to boil, turn off the burner and add the Borax and washing soda. Stir to dissolve.

2. In a large bucket (I use a 2-gallon bucket from the hardware store), combine the remaining 11 cups of room-temperature water and 1 cup Dr. Bronner's Liquid Soap.

3. Add the essential oil scent of your choice (optional).

4. Pour the hot Borax mixture from the saucepan

into the bucket.

5. Stir the mixture together.

6. Pour your mixture into any desired storage container.

7. As the soap sits, the mixture may form into a gel. There may also be liquid and gel separation; simply stir or shake. This is normal. You can use 1/8-1/4 a cup of soap per load of laundry.

Vinegar and Baking Soda: These ingredients work together, and they will help get the grime off of surfaces in your home that aren't being cleaned with hot water or other methods, things like countertops and floors.

There are many things that you can do to help save money on your home cleaning budget.

Cleaning routines
Everyone has a different idea of how they like their house to be cleaned. Here are some great cleaning routines that you can use in your home that are pocketbook-friendly while maintaining a clean, serene environment

Weekly: Once a week, you should be cleaning the main areas of your home, like the kitchen, living room, bedroom, and bathroom. You can also do this in areas that are hard to get to if it makes you feel more comfortable about it. If you stay on top of your cleaning routine, you'll only be spending a couple of hours accomplishing these tasks.

Monthly: Once per month you should deep clean all of the rooms in your home to make sure that they look great when you are finished with them. The sink and all kitchen appliances should be cleaned, and you should clean the tiles on the floor if you have any, and vacuum carpets and rugs from dirt and dust build-up. Did you know that dust is a build-up of people's skin cells, hair, clothing fibers, bacteria, dust mites, bits of dead bugs, soil particles, pollen, and microscopic specks of plastic? When you see layers of this build-up on furniture, tables and inanimate objects, it's kind of gross to think about when you're cleaning, but your home looks so much brighter and fresher when the dust is removed

Every Six Months: This is more of an aesthetic thing that is really only good for your overall health rather than anything else. You should check that the floors are looking good, move furniture around to clean under them, check the grout in all of your bathrooms, and make sure that all rugs are washed. You're only spending a few hours doing this, so it's not a huge chore.

Yearly: Once per year, it's nice to get your carpets cleaned professionally. This will help keep them clean and fresh-looking for a long time so that you don't have to worry about it.

Deep Cleaning: This is more of an in-depth cleaning that is meant to get rid of all the dust and grime that has built up over time. This is usually done every year, so it's not too bad if you want to give your home a good cleaning once per year.

Spring Cleaning: During the winter when it's cold, sometimes clutter builds up. All the build-up of winter stuff and holiday items can get ignored until it starts warming up. It's time to do something about it. Spring cleaning is basically all the tasks that need to be done that you've procrastinated about all winter. These tasks need to be addressed in the spring in order to get your home ready for the spring and summer months. This is also sort of a reset for the year. Out with the old, in with the new.

Do the Laundry

Remember the good ol' days when your mom or dad would come in and take all your clothes and wash and fold them? Remember that smell of freshly washed and folded wardrobe? Well, now it's all on you to make those smells and nicely folded laundry a reality. No more parents interrupting the thing you wanted to do as they demanded you to clean your room and do your laundry. You have to demand it for yourself. Laundry doesn't have to be done every day if you have enough laundry to last you all week. It's best to schedule time to wash, dry, then fold the laundry. If you're fortunate enough to have a washer and dryer in your home, this is a good money saver. If you do not, then you need to make sure you budget enough to take your laundry to the cleaners or a laundromat.

Don't destroy your clothes, check the labels:

If you aren't sure if a product or a wash cycle could destroy your clothes, look at the label. If it says "dry clean only" or "hand wash only," then that probably means that a standard washing machine or dryer is going to be bad for your clothing. You should also check the back of your clothing to see if there is anything on it that can tell you more about what you can and cannot do with them.

Using a machine clothes washer

A machine washer is a good way to get your clothes clean, but it can be too harsh on them if you aren't careful. There are steps that you can take to make sure that you are not overdoing it, and that your clothes will look great longer because of it.

Prewash: It's important that you prewash anything new before putting them through the wash. This will help remove any loose dirt or staining so that they don't end up damaging your clothes.

Don't overfill: It's always important to make sure that you aren't overfilling your machine. If you do, the agitation will be too much for your garments and they will wear down faster.

Use a softener: You should use a softener on your clothes if you want them to last as long as possible. This is because it will be gentler on the fibers and help them to last longer.

Remove Stains

If you have a stain on your clothes, you can use a variety of methods to remove them. It's important to do this as soon as possible because otherwise, it might start to set in permanently. These methods have been shown to work for the most stubborn of stains and will be able to remove them efficiently so that they don't ruin your clothes anymore.

Lemon Juice: If you have a white shirt with red wine stains on it, then this method is going to take it out if you use it right away. You should pour pure lemon juice on the stain using a spoon and let that sit for thirty minutes or so before washing it in cold water. The lemon juice will break down the stain and make it easier for you to get it out of your garment.

Soft Scrub: If you have a grease stain on your shirt, then you should try to use some Soft Scrub on it. All you need to do is scrub the Soft Scrub right into the spot, and then wash as normal. This should loosen up most stains and make them much easier to remove.

Ammonia: You should be careful when using this method because ammonia can be really bad for clothing but if your spot is white or light-colored, then you can try using this method with ammonia. Note: ammonia can alter the color of colored fabric so don't apply to dark colors.

Chapter Seven

Healthy Cooking And Food Skills

M any say that eating healthy is the best way to get through life, but when you're on a budget, things can be a bit tough. So, what do you do if you have limited income, are living alone or with one other person, and need to make dinners that are cheap, healthy, yet satisfying? How do you prepare food that can be multiplied into more meals, i.e., casseroles, spaghetti, sandwiches, etc.?

Eating healthy doesn't have to break the bank. It can be done. There is a myth out there that cooking is expensive, but these tips will help you spend less while eating healthy by saving money, by buying the right ingredients, making smart menu choices, and making the most of leftovers. Let's start with some basic food skills.

Saving money on food doesn't just mean saving money on groceries; it also means saving money on dining out. The quality of the food served at restaurants isn't that good for you and is usually overpriced for what you get. You can make a better meal for yourself by cooking at home and having leftovers that you can use later in the week.

Most restaurants have "specials" or multiple-item meals because they are always looking to sell you more food than you need. You may spend $5 to $10 extra because of this, so it's best to avoid eating out unless you're getting a great deal (like happy hour).

Saving money on food isn't hard if you start saving money on dining out. You can cook for yourself at home or start making multiple meals (like casseroles and stir fry) that you can use throughout the week. Start small and take it one step at a time so you don't get overwhelmed with your food budget!

What are "Best Before" dates and "Used by Dates"?

The best-before date is the most common distinction between fresh produce and flour. The best-before date is the date when your produce is no longer safe to eat. Most fresh fruits and vegetables have a shelf life of a couple of weeks, while some types of flour have a shelf life that is limited to about 6 months (this depends on the quality).

Used-by dates are another important symbol for knowing when foods should be thrown out. These are the dates that the food item should be eaten or thrown out.

Once you throw food of either of these two categories in the garbage, it can attract contaminants and smell. So keep this in mind when you toss them in the trash vs. how long it will be before you take the trash out. You can also store food for disposal in the freezer until you're ready to take out the trash.

How to clean food

There is no need to purchase expensive cleaners, just wash your produce thoroughly with cold water and dry it with a paper towel before eating, no matter how organic or conventionally grown. Do not use soap when cleaning fruits and vegetables because the porous surfaces on fresh produce can absorb the ingredients of soap. After rinsing off fresh lettuce, rinse it with cold water because this will slow down the bacteria growth. Fruits with indigestible peels such as bananas, watermelons, oranges, and avocados, still need to be washed. Even if the peel will not be eaten, there could be dirt and bacteria that can be transferred from the peel to the fruit inside when it's sliced or peeled.

If you're wondering if you should wash raw poultry, beef, pork, lamb or veal before cooking, it is not recommended. A simple rinse with cold water is sufficient to remove excess juices from the meat. Decades ago, washing meat was appropriate; however, the modern food safety system doesn't require it any longer. At the same time, be careful that bacteria in raw meat and poultry juices can be spread to other foods, utensils and surfaces. You have to be careful of cross-contamination.

Freezer Storage

You might be someone who does not have the time to cook daily or who might have to work long shifts. Eating fast food or having food delivered can be a tempting solution, but it's not the healthiest choice and is usually not the most budget-friendly option, either. One of the best budget-friendly food prepping you can do is utilize your freezer. You can stock up your freezer with fresh or frozen food, or prep meals for the week for when you need it instead of going out all the time.

When first putting your food in the freezer, make sure that you use tightly sealed plastic bags. Put all of your food into freezer bags to protect it from freezer burn. It's also a good idea to write the date on the bags that you're putting in the freezer, so you will know how long something has been stored. Frozen food and meals will remain usable for months without spoiling. If possible, it's best to place foods with a higher risk of foodborne illnesses like meats near the back of the freezer where the temperature is more consistent and colder.

Fruits and vegetables

Fruits and vegetables are essential for a healthy diet, but can sometimes be difficult to store properly. Most refrigerators have a bin for storing fruits and vegetables, which utilizes low humidity to keep produce fresher for longer. This will extend their shelf life by 3 to 5 days.

If you have a lot of fruits and vegetables that you need to store, there are several options:

Refrigerator

Keep your fruits and vegetables on a tray at the bottom of your refrigerator. This is the coldest part in the refrigerator. Make sure it's not directly under a vent since this will cause them to spoil quickly.

Antimicrobial Produce Bags

These bags are great for storing produce such as apples, pears, bell peppers, and more. The bags cost about $4.00 and will extend produce shelf life by up to 20%. The bags have an active ingredient that is formulated to prevent the growth of fungus and molds.

Any fruit or vegetable can be placed in these bags, as long as they are washed first before being put in the bags. You can purchase these bags at any grocery store or online through Amazon.

Meats

Protein is important in a well-balanced diet, but protein can be expensive. Purchasing in large quantities can be very budget friendly if you're going to store them in a freezer for later use or cook up meals for the week and store them in the refrigerator. If you're going to store meat in the freezer. You'll want to make sure you remove the meat from the original package. Dry it using a paper towel to remove excess liquid from the surface. Then place it in a dry airtight container/glass container, a freezer bag with little air in it, or wrapped in freezer paper.

The Benefits:

1) Healthy source of protein.

2) Easy to make at home.

3) Easy to cook on a weekly basis.

4) Can be frozen for later use.

Bread

Making bread isn't that hard, but it does take many hours for it to rise (about 1 hour per loaf of bread). This is why it's much easier to cook up a full batch of homemade bread than just one or two pieces. Homemade bread is much cheaper than the loaves you find at the grocery store, and there's nothing like fresh warm bread from the oven. The ingredients for homemade bread are much cheaper too.

The Benefits:

1) You can make as much bread dough as you want and it will last for up to 1 week in the fridge. The best way to make this homemade bread is to freeze half of it so you can eat fresh bread every day.

2) It's healthier because there are no preservatives added to it.

3) It costs less than store-bought bread and the ingredients are cheaper.

4) It's more convenient because you can make as much bread dough as you want and freeze part of it.

Here is a simple bread recipe to get you started. You can find many recipes other online.

Ingredients
5 3/4 to 6 1/4 cups all-purpose flour or bread flour (range of flour depends on how humid or dry your

baking day is) 1 package dry yeast 2 1/4 cups milk 2 tablespoons sugar 1 tablespoon butter 1 1/2 teaspoons salt Combine 2 1/2 cups flour and yeast; set aside.

In either a saucepan on the stove or a good-sized microwavable bowl in the microwave, heat and stir the milk, sugar, butter, and salt to just lukewarm (120 degrees) and the butter is starting to melt.

Add milk mixture to flour mixture. Mix until good elastic gluten is formed and well blended. Using a wooden spoon, stir in as much of the remaining flour as you can. Turn the dough out onto a floured surface. Knead in enough of the remaining flour to make a moderately stiff dough that is smooth and elastic (about 8 minutes).

Place dough in a lightly greased bowl, turning once to grease the surface of the dough. Cover; let rise in a warm place until double in size (about an hour, depending on how warm your house is). NOTE: Do not let rise in too warm a space or you will have big holes in your bread from rising too fast. Punch the dough in the middle with your fist to let the air out. (Punching the dough has been my favorite part since I was a kid when my mother made bread). Turn dough out onto a lightly floured surface; divide in half.

Cover; let rest for 10 minutes. Meanwhile, lightly grease two 8x4x2 bread pans. Take each section of dough and roll it out with a rolling pin to pop bubbles. Roll tightly into a loaf shape, pinching dough to secure the seam and pulling ends together at the seam. Place shaped dough into bread pans, turning once to grease both sides. Cover and let rise in a warm place until nearly double (30 to 40 minutes). Bake at 375 degrees for about 30 minutes or until bread sounds hollow when lightly tapped. Immediately remove the bread from the pan and onto a cooling rack. Using a pastry brush, brush butter on the bread tops to keep the crust soft. Cool before slicing, and enjoy.

Breakfast

You probably wake up in the morning and instantly think, "Coffee." Well, this is not good for you. Coffee isn't really good for you unless you only drink a few cups a day (less than three), but if you have more, it can lead to dehydration which can lead to an early death. If you just don't want to drink water or tea in the morning, then make yourself some eggs, sausage, and toast. Eggs are another breakfast food that most people overlook because of the cholesterol content, but they are actually good for your body when eaten in moderation (1 egg per day).

Chapter Eight

Maintaining Your Mode of Transportation

For most people, getting around without relying on others is a necessity. Unless you have the option of taking a taxi, bus, tram, or subway everyday, you need to get from point A to point B. You need to be able to get to and from work on time, and a personal car is an important tool for you. Are you thinking of owning a car? There are a lot of really cool cars out there, but if you're just starting out and you don't have a lot of money, then you shouldn't be going after the flashy expensive cars with all the bells and whistles. You need to look for something that is reliable, as well as something that isn't going to break down every month costing you loads of money you don't have. Go for fuel efficiency: A car that gets over 30 MPG is where you should be looking; maybe a hybrid or electric car. If you can find a car that will get you on average above 30 MPG, you'll be able to keep your gas budget low.

Cars can be expensive. Car repairs can be even more draining on finances, and they always seem to come at the worst possible time. Knowing how to do simple maintenance to your car can save hundreds of dollars down the road. Learning these essential skills can help you avoid the financial burden that comes with owning a car

Car skills everyone should know

Here are a few handy skills that everyone should know how to do.

How to fill a gas tank

Something I took for granted, thinking the one thing everyone knew was how to put gas into the car. I was rudely awakened the day I asked one of my teenagers to fill my gas tank. First, they looked at me like I had lost my mind as if to say, "Dad, how stupid do you think I am?" I wanted to see if they could figure it out without me telling them what to do. So, I got out of the car, handed them my debit card and said go for it. It was funny to watch them walk around the car looking for the gas tank, then try to figure out how to open the gas tank. It got even more humorous to watch them figure out how to pay at the pump. With some frustration on their part, and little hints from me, they managed to figure it out, and I bet they won't forget the lesson in the future.

One thing that many people never think to check is how full the tank is. I can't tell you how many times I got into my wife's car to run an errand to find out the car is on empty. I'm given just enough gas to barely make it to the gas station. I personally like to be more prepared than this. I always think what if there are delays on the road? What if there is some sort of emergency? I would recommend that you either fill up when you're at half or a quarter tank. You'll spend less at the pump because you're not filling the car up from E, but also if an emergency happens or you don't have time to go to the gas station, you'll be assured you'll have some gas in your car at all times.

Which side of the car is your gas tank on? Many people don't realize that in just about every car, the gas gauge shows you which side the gas tank is on. This helps when you are trying to figure out which way to pull up next to the pump. On the gas gauge there is an icon of a gas pump. On either the left or right side there is an arrow pointing to which side of the car the gas tank is on.

What are the differences between gases?

You've probably noticed at the gas station there are more than one gas option. Premium, Regular, and Super Unleaded. The difference in these is how much octane there is in the gas. Octane is how much compression a fuel can withstand before igniting, or rather it's a measurement of a fuel's ability to avoid a knock in your engine. This is why high-end luxury cars need to use Premium (High Octane) when they fuel up. Gas stations typically carry three octane grades. State laws regulate which octane levels can be listed as premium, mid-grade or regular. Typically "regular" gas is 87 octane, "mid-grade" is 89 octane, and over 91 octane is "premium" gasoline. Some states label top-tier gasoline with 93 octane as "ultra" gas.

The general consensus is that using premium gas when your car can run on regular gas doesn't deliver any extra benefits when it comes to engine life, fuel economy, or reduced emissions. So, if your car can run on cheaper gas, use the cheaper gas.

Ethanol vs. Ethanol-free gas You will find that most gas stations have Ethanol mixed gas. You might find it options to have 10% or 15% Ethanol gas. Ethanol is an alcohol-based biodegradable mixture added to the gas and is made from corn. You will be able to tell how much Ethanol is in your gas by looking for an E10 or E15 on the pump.

If you see at the pump Ethanol free, that means you're getting pure gasoline. The advantages of Ethonal free gas is that it offers better gas mileage and won't rust out your engine parts because Ethonal by nature attracts water and we all know what water does to metal over time. Ethanol free gas can be a tad more expensive so the choice is yours on if you want to use it and how often you want to use it.

Checking oil

The engine is one of the most critical systems in your vehicle, and you need to ensure that everything is operating correctly. Checking the oil in your car is one of the most important things to do if you want to keep it running well. If you care about the performance of your car, you should know how to check engine oil. It's not that complicated, and the rewards are worth it – you can save a lot of money and trouble by knowing what to look for.

To check the health and oil levels of your car, you should do it while the engine is cold. This will not only keep the pressure off the system, but it will also help you from possibly getting burned. Locate the oil dipstick. If you do not know where this is for your car, you can probably look in the car manual or Google it. Make sure you have a paper towel or something handy to wipe off the oil off the dipstick the first time you pull it out. You do this to get an accurate reading of oil levels. With the now dry dipstick, insert it back into place and pull it out again. This time look at the very end of the stick. There should be a marker at the end of the stick that will say if you're full or empty. Depending on where your fluid level is to the full line will tell you how much oil you need, if at all. The second thing you want to look for is how dirty the oil is. The cleaner the oil, the clearer it will look. You might not be able to tell just by looking at the dipstick (especially if the oil is clean), so while the stick is out, use the paper towel and look at what color is left on the towel. If it's brownish, that means an oil change will be needed soon. If it's black, it's time to take it to the shop to get it changed. Naturally, clean fresh oil is clear with a tint of yellow.

Every time you take your car to get an oil change, the mechanic should put a sticker on the inside of your windshield with a mileage number to remind you when your mileage meter reaches this number, it will be time for an oil change again. On average, you will need to have your oil changed every 5,000 - 7,500 miles. If you find that you are running low on oil or the oil gets black way before 5,000 miles, you might have something else going on. You could be burning oil or leaking it. Either way, you'll need to inform your mechanic about this so they can do a deeper investigation into what's going on with the engine. If you don't check the oil often, you potentially could ruin the engine without the proper amount of oil or clean enough oil. This can be quite expensive to repair and very dangerous because it can cause problems with your car.

Checking your coolant

Checking how much coolant your car has is also very important. You need to check your engine's coolant at least twice a year, usually once at the beginning of summer and at the beginning of winter. Coolant keeps the motor from overheating and allows it to work properly. If you don't keep an eye on how much coolant your car has, you are putting yourself at risk for overheating which can cause your engine to burn up and even become a hazard for a potential crash.

It's also important to know that you must have the right amount of liquid in your car for it to run properly. Ensure your car is running correctly before checking the fluid level because too much or too little can throw off the working conditions and make it dangerous.

If you have any coolant leaks, take your car to a mechanic as soon as possible so they can figure out the cause. You don't want to be stranded on the side of the road with an overheated car because you underestimated how much coolant the car was using.

You do not want to drive around with a coolant leak. Coolant fluid is flammable and could catch on fire from the heat and could cause an accident or worse, so you should make sure that things are being looked after properly.

Checking windshield wipers and fluid

Wiper blades are another item that most people forget about, but they are essential to overall visibility and safety when driving your car.

You're going to want to check and make sure that there is enough wiper fluid in the car before going out for long trips. The more you drive, the more often you should check it. If road dirt or debris lands on your windshield and obstructs your field of vision, you need something that can fix this quickly. Wiper fluid has a component that not only helps remove sticky bug guts, but it also can help rain bead up and leave the windshield faster. If your wipers are getting old, they can leave streaks obstructing your view and they might not remove pesky gunk from the windshield.

Checking the car's air filter

Your car's engine has an air filter. This filter protects your engine from being damaged by dust, dirt, sand, and other debris that gets kicked up while driving. If this filter becomes clogged and starts suffocating the airflow an engine needs, it can impact your car's performance. Some mechanics will try to get you to change your air filter every time you change your oil. It doesn't hurt to change it often, but it's an unneeded expense if you don't really need to have it changed. You should check your car's air filter at least every six months to keep your engine running at optimal performance.

Changing lights

Changing your headlights and taillights is an essential and straightforward maintenance process that you should always check. This is especially true when you are driving in heavy traffic or if you are planning on going out after dark.

This process can be a little tricky, so it's best to read online guides to help you out and get some tools to make the job easier for yourself.

Jumpstarting a car

If your battery has gone dead, then there is nothing better than using jumper cables. These cables are reusable and don't cost a lot of money, so they are worth obtaining before having a problem with your car's battery. It's always a good idea to have these in your car for an emergency for yourself or to help out a fellow neighbor if they are having car trouble. If you can learn how to jump-start a car, then you have the potential to save yourself money on a tow truck or being stranded. This can also help ease the stress of having your car break down because you won't have to worry about not being able to call a friend, family member, or roadside assistance.

If you're not sure how to jump-start your car, don't worry. It's a pretty easy process that we'll walk you through step by step!

First things first. If you don't have jumper cables, you'll need to find someone who has a good set of jumper cables and is in good physical shape. Then, park the cars close enough so one end of the jumper cables will be able to reach from your car battery to the other person's car battery. Put the cars in park so they don't go rolling off when the engine starts. A jumper cable usually has two colors, black and red. This helps you know which end goes to the negative side of the battery (black) and which end of the jumper cable goes to the positive side of the battery (red). Usually on the battery next to the battery stems, there is a (+) symbol for positive and a (-) symbol for negative.

You can also tell by looking at the cables that are already connected to the battery which is which because the positive side cables will be red and the negative will be black. Start by connecting the black jumper cable to the negative stem of the battery from your car to the other person's car. Then proceed to connect the red cable to the positive side of the battery from your car to the other person's car. Be sure you DO NOT put the incorrect jumper cable on the incorrect side of the battery. If this happens, you can cause damage to your electrical system or the other person's car electrical system.

If you've gone through all that but still can't get your car to start, then you might have to take out your battery and take it to a store to check to see if the battery can be recharged. If it can't, the battery will probably need to be replaced. If you've done all the above and you know the battery is good and has a charge and your car still won't start, then it's time to get it to a mechanic to see if the problem is elsewhere.

Take care of your tires

Wheels are also an important part of your car and if they aren't taken care of, then you could end up with a flat tire or have to have your car towed somewhere. It's recommended to check the pressure of your tires about every two to four weeks. You always want to make sure you have proper tire pressure before going on long road trips or if you're going to be towing or carrying heavy loads. Planning ahead will keep you from getting stuck on the side of the road and being stranded. Doing this will save yourself a lot of money because a tow truck is much more expensive than checking the air pressure on your tires.

You'll want to know the proper amount of PSI (pound-force per square inch) your tire needs to run safely and optimally. On average, most tires will need about 32 - 40 PSI of air. If you are unsure how to know for sure, you can talk to a mechanic, Google your tire by brand and model number, or ask the people who sold you the tires. Adding air in your tires is very simple. Most gas stations have an air pump with a tire pressure gauge attached to the hose. It's really no different than putting air in your bicycle tires. You take the cap of the air valve, attach the air pressure hose to it, and pump in the air.

Rotate your tires

As you ride on your tires, the rubber gets worn down. If you drive at the same times in the same position for a very long time, the tires get worn down in the same place which can degrade the tire tread faster. It can also wear the tire down so much in one place, it can make the tire so weak in that area it will pop or blow out which is extremely dangerous at high speeds.

So how do you maximize the life of your tires? You have the tires rotated, meaning you have a mechanic move the front tires to the back and the back tires to the front and swap the side the tire was on to the other side of the car. (It's recommended you have your tires rotated every 5,000 - to 7,500 miles.)

Change a tire

There are many different things that can happen to your car while you are driving. The further you drive, the more likely it is that something will go wrong. One of the common things you will have happen to you at some point in your life in dealing with vehicles is having to change a tire. It's always a good idea to make sure you have the proper and correct supplies stored safely in your vehicle.

Here are some quick tips to make sure you're prepared in case of an emergency and need to change out a tire:

1. Make sure you have a spare that is in good condition and has the proper tire pressure.

2. Make sure you know how to remove your spare tire from its storage place. Some vehicles have some tricky ways they store spare tires.

3. Make sure you have a jack that is strong enough to lift your car easily and that you know how to use it.

4. Make sure you have a proper lug wrench that fits your lug nuts.

5. Make sure you have a flashlight. If you have work in the dark, this comes in really handy and is better than trying to use the flashlight on your phone.

6. A few other items that are not necessities but will make it easier to do this work would be gloves, a rain poncho, and a mat for kneeling.

How to change a tire

1. If it is possible, try to find a safe place to pull over. Make sure that you're off the road where you won't be hit by traffic, but also that your car is on stable ground so you can use a jack effectively. If the ground is too soft, you may not be able to jack up your car to get the tire removed.

2. Turn on your hazard lights so people can tell from a far distance that there is a car in distress so

they have plenty of time to react, slow down, and provide you distance so there won't be a chance they will hit you.

3. Put your car in Park and apply your parking brake. You do not want your car moving on you at any point during this procedure.

4. Set up your jack and make sure as you raise your car that you have the jack set to use the metal frame of the car. The frame is the most stable part of the car to hold the weight of the car. If you have trouble locating the proper place, your car's user manual will also be able to help you locate the right place to position the jack. If you do not use the metal frame when raising the car, you could damage your car or it could come crashing down on you causing even more damage to your car and possibly do you bodily harm.

5. Once your car is lifted off the ground, you can proceed to remove the lug nuts. The lug nuts will need to be turned counterclockwise until they are very loose. You will want to keep all the nuts together so they don't get lost as you will be using them again to secure the spare tire to the car.

6. Take the spare and align the holes of the spare to the lug posts and slide the spare on, pushing it as far onto the wheelbase as possible.

7. As you replace the lug nuts, you will want to tighten them by hand and in increments, alternating every other nut. As an example, you'll want to mentally number the lug stems 1,2,3,4,5. As you put the lug nuts on you will put them on 1,3,5,2,4 and you will tighten them in that order as well, 1,3,5,2,4.

8. After they are hand tightened as best as you can, you can lower the car down and then completely tighten the lug nuts using the lug wrench and following the 1,3,5,2,4 pattern. Make sure they are very tight when you are done as you do not want the spare to fall off while driving.

Sometimes your spare tire is not a full-size tire. It could be a smaller tire than the rest of your tires. If you have this type of spare tire, you do not want to drive very fast or very far as this tire is meant to get you to where you need to go to get your regular tire fixed. It's recommended to not go over 50 mph on a tire like this.

Cars are very important when it comes to our everyday lives, and most people will have to have one to get around. Today more than ever, you need to know how to manage the maintenance of your car so that you can keep it running for as long as possible. Not only this, but you will want to know how each part inside a car works to make sure that you are getting the most out of your driving experience.

It's also very important that you know how to check every little thing on your vehicle because not doing this can result in a huge problem or even death if this is neglected.

Final Words

I n my youth, my biggest mistake was my ego and not preparing myself to be independent. I was being a bit lax in planning, and that affected my ability to help myself. In most cases, it wasn't any real effort that I had to make to be independent. So, when times got a little rough and dirty, I had no idea how to cope. Back then, I didn't have the luxury of the internet to solve all my problems. I had to learn by failing. After failure, you tend to learn real quick how to protect yourself from that kind of pain and embarrassment in the future.

Therefore, I recommend that you take your time to plan ahead and then figure out how to use the resources around you to be independent. Not only can this be fun, but it also helps you develop discipline as well as a good work ethic. Another big mistake that I made was not taking the time to learn how to survive financially. If a financial emergency did come about, I would normally be left in the dark and unable to meet my needs until I could figure out a way to rise above the problem.

Having an emergency fund and developing a saving habit will come to the rescue. Starting these good habits early will be the best action to achieve independence. As you progress, I recommend that you keep a budget to track your spending and income. This will give you a clear picture of how to use up your money (especially if an emergency occurs), and it will also teach you how to save money. And if you don't have a budget, that may be another mistake that you need to make in order to achieve financial independence.

Keep in mind that living alone means all financial burdens are borne by you. Buying necessities like groceries and clothes at discounts save you money which will come in handy to your survival. I also highly recommend that you take the time to do some financial planning to get yourself set up for material security in the future. There are several things that can be done in order to have a better income in the future, but it is important that someone begins thinking about these things now rather than later.

I learned how to be self-reliant through trial and error. It was a lot of hard work, failure, and determination, but for me it was worth it. I don't recommend it for everyone, which is why I wrote this book in hopes it will help you avoid some of the pitfalls out there.

Remember that you have resources all around you. Sometimes, we take these resources for granted, and then when the time comes that we actually need them, they are not available to us. In order to avoid this situation, I recommend that you slowly work your way through your plan and then make sure that you use these resources to their full extent. I suggest that you take your time and do it right the first time. By doing this, you will have a better foundation for learning new skills, which can come in handy for almost anything.

Break down your plan into steps and small actions, so they are easy to complete one by one. Once you have started, continue on until the task is complete rather than leaving things up in the air.

I hope that this book will help you gain the confidence you need to succeed in making your own way. Good luck, and stay focused on what's important; learning how to handle money as an adult will be difficult, but with hard work and perseverance, you can overcome any obstacles!

A great way to learn to be self-reliant is through experience. However, if you happen to have an outdated or poor-quality set of skills that are no longer useful, then it may be best to look into the possibility of getting them updated. It is not something that should be done in a rush. Therefore, it is crucial that you take your time if you are trying to keep learning something new.

Friendly Reminder

THANK YOU FOR READING!

You are awesome and I know you'll do great on your own.

I would like to ask you a small favor. If you enjoyed this book and think others will benefit from it, would you please consider writing an honest REVIEW on Amazon?

Your review will inspire me to keep writing these kinds of books that will help you get the results you want.

Writing a review is one of the best ways to support the work of independent authors like me. It would mean a lot.

Thank you!

SOMETHING FOR YOU!

Get your <u>FREE</u> pre-built budget/bank reconciliation calculator

GET YOUR COPY

https://dadtothebone.com/budgetguide

Acknowledgments

Cover Art:

This cover has been designed using assets from Freep ik.com
Freepik. (2020, December 16). *Businessman at laptop and leader runs up on books with trophy and his team. business leadership, managing skills, leadership training plan concept. pinkish coral bluevector isolated illustration Free Vector.* https://www.freepik.com/free-vector/businessman-la ptop-leader-runs-up-books-with-trophy-his-team-bu siness-leadership-managing-skills-leadership-training -plan-concept-pinkish-coral-bluevector-isolated-illust ration_11667110.htm

Made in the USA
Monee, IL
16 December 2023

49461367R00098